Fresh Ideas for
DISCIPLESHIP & NURTURE

fresh ideas

FOR

DISCIPLESHIP & NURTURE

WORD BOOKS
PUBLISHER
WACO, TEXAS

A DIVISION OF
WORD, INCORPORATED

Christianity Today, Inc.
Carol Stream, Illinois

Edited by Dean Merrill and Marshall Shelley
Designed by Tim Botts

© 1982, 1983, 1984 Christianity Today, Inc.
Published by Christianity Today, Inc.
465 Gundersen Drive, Carol Stream, IL 60188
Printed in the United States of America
ISBN 0-917463-02-1

CONTENTS

INTRODUCTION 7

DISCIPLESHIP 9

Happy Birthday, New Christian! . . . Stated Expectations . . .
Feature: *New Disciples: Born, but Also Made . . . A Notebook for
Growing . . . The Witness Stand . . . A Word from the Pew . . .
Dads Who Mean Business . . .* Feature: *Where Family Devotions Are
Alive and Well . . . A Big Push for Small Groups . . . Home Bible
Studies: What to Do with the Kids . . .* Feature: *Honing the Two-
Edged Sword . . . The Day a Chain Saw Came to Church . . .*
Feature: *Helping Christians Go to Work . . . A Start Worth Honoring
. . . Worship Away from Home . . .* Feature: *Where the Divorced
Get More Than Sympathy*

PRAYER 49

*Sharing That Edifies . . . Secret Intercessors . . . Who Will Pray? . . .
A Tracking System for Prayer Requests . . . Prayer: The Proof Is in the
Doing . . . The Prayer Connection . . . Pray Now, Pray Later . . .
Welding Stronger Prayer Chains . . . Remembering to Pray . . . Testi-
monies in Stereo . . . Believers' Checkbook . . .* Feature: *Ministering to
the Sick on Sunday Morning . . .* Feature: *Anyone for Fasting? Well,
Yes . . .*

EDUCATION 71

*Peace in the Adult Department . . . An Easy Way to Increase Sun-
day School . . . Baskin-Robbins Bible Study . . . Recasting an Old Tradi-
tion . . . A Guest Who Needs No Introduction . . . No More
Anonymous Teachers . . . For Adults: a Piece of the Action . . . What Do
Teachers Do? . . .* Feature: *Why We Moved Sunday School to Satur-
day . . . Tertullian Who? . . . A Class That Spells Relief . . . Layers of
Bible Study: Reinforced, Concrete . . . Adults Enjoy Back Yards, Too
. . . Downtown Devotion . . . An Upbeat Start for Couples' Classes*

SERVING 95

"What Would You LIKE to Do?" . . . Church Is a Many-Splendored Thing . . . Feature: Staying Close with All the Members . . . Deacons on Call . . . Sharing the Abundance . . . Lending More Than an Ear . . . The People Bank . . . Quick with a Quiche . . . The Moving Crew . . . Where Needs Get Action . . . Round Trip Guaranteed . . . Humbling Yourself in the Sight of the Town . . . Working Wonders . . . The Job Finders . . . Feature: No Wings, but a Lot of Prayer . . . Youth and Adults in Action . . . Feature: Prisoners on the Loose

COUNSELING 127

Self-Service Disclosure . . . Making the Most of Counseling Time . . . To Charge or Not to Charge . . . A Professional Next Door . . . A Missing Link in Counseling . . . Images That Heal . . . Learning from the Pros . . . Feature: Outside Assignments in Premarital Counseling . . . Individual Group Therapy . . . When to Stop Counseling

FELLOWSHIP 141

Scrambled Eggs, Scrambled Ages . . . Blessings in a Bag . . . Food for the Body and the Spirit . . . Dinners for Six . . . The No-Hassle Guest List . . . A Pumped-up Party . . . Invite-a-Member-to-Dinner Sunday . . . King-Sized Compliment . . . Honoring the Unsung . . . Encouragement Sunday . . . Sowing a Crop of Compliments . . . Year-Round Cheer . . . Postal Prayers . . . Push-Button Visitation . . . Pastoral Visits: What to Talk About . . . They Don't Miss This Bulletin Board . . . Circles Yes, Cliques No . . . Anybody Need a Toaster? . . . The Hospitality Basket . . . Feature: Stewardship Means More Than $$$ . . . When Members Move Away: a Consolation . . . Feature: Good Mourning

OLDER ADULTS 173

Sunday Grannies . . . A Crew for You . . . A Fragrant Offering . . . A Mission Trip for 70-Year-Olds . . . Demythologizing Cancer . . . Project YOU (Young and Old United) . . . The Telecare Club . . . Shut-in but Not Shut Out . . . Ma Bell's Call to Worship . . . The Communion of Elder Saints . . . See What He Means? . . . Never Too Old to Learn . . . A Harvest of Years . . . An Object Lesson for the Dying

INTRODUCTION

Welcome to a smorgasbord of fresh ideas for the local church.

This book — and the other three in the series — have been created to give pastors and lay leaders solutions. Few problems in church life are unique; most challenges have cropped up somewhere else — and been conquered. It's only logical, then, to share creative answers with one another. If a solution has already been tried and proven in Gainesville or Rochester, why reinvent it in Ponca City?

Contrary to popular opinion, there *is* innovation and creativity in the churches across the United States and Canada. This book showcases that creativity.

As you read the many short vignettes and the longer features, you'll find some that contain several ideas you can use, others only one. Sometimes a single sentence will trigger a brainstorm with which you can attack a particular problem you're facing. The point is not to swallow these ideas whole but rather to tailor them to your situation, adapting, modifying, and even improving as you go.

Most of the reports here were first published during 1982-83 in a magazine called *Leadership 100*. Similar material from *Leadership* Journal has been added to this collection. While not all ideas may be still in place as described here, and no doubt there have been personnel changes in some churches, we believe the value of the ideas stands intact.

As you read, enjoy the good news that churches are doing some things *right* — and help yourself to the creativity, which has its ultimate source not in any human mind but in God alone.

DEAN MERRILL
Senior Editor, *Leadership*

DISCIPLESHIP

Happy Birthday, New Christian!

If the angels rejoice when a new person joins God's family, how about the earthly brothers and sisters, too?

That's exactly what happens at Highland Park Church of Christ, an inner-city congregation in Los Angeles. Approximately every three weeks "spiritual birthday parties" are held after a Sunday evening service to honor those who have recently come to Christ.

The Dixon (Ill.) Church of Christ does a similar thing each quarter in the form of a "Super Sunday Celebration" — a midday potluck on the fifth Sunday of months that have one.

"We believe a disciple's new birth is at least as important as physical birth," says William Pile, one of the California church's three pastors.

"So within a few days of one's baptism, we throw a party.

"First, following the evening service (which we usually cut a little short), we interview the new Christians; this gives the whole group a window into their lives and personalities. Then we invite the older Christians to share Scriptural insights, favorite helpful passages, poems, and personal wisdom that will aid the new believers in living up to their commitment to Jesus. Our people are really quite spontaneous at this. We ask everyone to address their comments directly to the new disciples.

"Then, we move to the fellowship area for cake, cookies, punch, and coffee. During this time, older Christians are urged to spend a few moments with each new Christian to make him or her feel welcome and loved."

Such celebrations help weld the church's various ethnic groups together. "The church is predominantly Latin, and we Anglos sometimes aren't thought to be friendly," Pile explains. "The spiritual birthday party really loosens everyone up to enjoy one another. It also reminds everyone of how often God is working in people's lives, bringing them to salvation."

Stated Expectations

Churches that practice believer's baptism often ask people, before they're immersed, to publicly declare their desire "to walk in newness of life."

But at First Assembly of God in Jamestown, North Dakota, the "fine print" of the new life is specifically stated.

"At the time of baptism, I ask each candidate to promise four things," says Pastor Jack Glass.

● To regularly attend the services of the church.

● To live a consistent Christian life.

● To seek opportunities to share the faith with others.

● To support the church with tithes and offerings.

"The benefits have been outstanding," says Glass. "As each candidate stands in the baptistry, his vows become a sermon to the entire congregation. And 99 percent of our new members begin immediately to tithe and give offerings.

"This has certainly helped new believers come more quickly into maturity in their Christian walk."

NEW DISCIPLES: BORN, BUT ALSO MADE

by Gary Olsby, minister of Christian education, West Valley Christian Church, Canoga Park, California

It has become fashionable these days for churches to preach "disciple making." Everyone is for it. Everyone claims it as a priority. The words, however, often exceed the reality.

A tragic personal experience made the need for disciple making a passion with me.

Several of my relatives attend the same church and had been trying for years to get my aunt involved. After much patient influence, she and her husband finally agreed to attend.

Following a couple of visits, the church leaders began sending people to their home each week on evangelistic visits. My aunt and her husband were impressed with people's concern; eventually they made decisions to follow Christ and to become church members. The tragedy: never again did anyone from the church contact them about spiritual things. As a result, they dropped out within a couple of years because they felt ignored. From their perspective, the church was concerned only with adding two more names to the membership rolls.

Churches cannot assume the job is done once someone makes a "decision" for Christ. We must fully incorporate each individual into the life of the church. And that job never ends.

In fact, author Lyle Schaller goes so far as to say, "It is un-Christian for a congregation to seek new members unless it is also willing and able to accept them into that called-out community."

Most Christians would agree with the need to help people grow into spiritual maturity. The question is how?

At West Valley Christian Church, we discovered an approach that has been amazingly effective, an approach that uses as its launching point an unlikely method: a study of Bible history.

Of course, the subject matter is merely the focus around which we gather. The other elements vital to making disciples — prayer, natural relationships with more mature Christians, the opportunity to ask practical questions, and the chance for new believers to share their own growing faith — are all part of the experience.

It began a few years ago when our staff, under the direction of Minister Glenn Kirby, began sensing that people didn't know Bible history. In Sunday school, references to the Babylonian exile brought blank stares. In sermons, mentioning the judges or Paul's imprisonment left people puzzled. We realized people couldn't fully understand any Bible text if they didn't know the historical settings.

Our strategy? A nine-month overview of Bible history for our adult Sunday school classes. We wrote our own curriculum, and the results surprised us. During those nine months, we gained 60 people in our Sunday school (we'd averaged 150 to that point), and after the class our people understood the basic story line of the Bible from Creation to the spread of the church.

But a new problem quickly arose. What do we do with newcomers? How do we provide them with this same solid foundation? Someone suggested we adapt the overview for one-on-one Bible study and use it for disciple making.

It worked. Led by Glenn Kirby's initiative and creativity, we put together a 61-page workbook, complete with maps and charts, to be taught in eight 1½-hour lessons. The workbook and the Bible would be the only tools necessary.

Next, we recruited people capable of teaching the material — not to a whole class, but to one or two others in their living rooms. Of those who'd completed the Sunday school class, 50 happily offered to pass along what they'd learned.

Many invited friends or neighbors to spend eight weekly sessions getting an overview of the Bible. If they couldn't find someone on their own, we introduced them to recent visitors to the church or others who wanted to brush up on the Bible.

Marty and Diane Young studied with the Lazenbys, a couple who had visited the church several times. The "eight-week" study began in January, but it was still going strong in June. Keith and Lynda Lazenby accepted Christ and were baptized during the time they were studying with the Youngs.

"We've found we've drawn closer not only to the Lord but also to each other," says Diane Young. "As Keith and Lynda learn more about God's will, they've become more active in church. Lynda now sings in the choir and comes with me to Thursday morning Bible study. My husband, Marty, baptized the entire family, and that was a special joy. After our overview study is complete, I pray that our friendship with Keith and Lynda will continue."

Rod and Rita White have also found the overview an effective tool in reaching non-Christians.

"We've had five separate studies with couples," says Rod, "and from four of them we've had conversions and baptisms. The overview gives people the understanding to make their own personal covenant with Christ."

One of the couples touched by the Whites was Bob and Bonny Setser.

"When Bonny and I came to West Valley," says Bob, "the Holy Spirit had just begun to make us aware of our spiritual needs. Bonny came from a totally nonreligious home, and I'd turned away from the church in my late teens. But we both felt a void in our lives and wondered if the Lord could fill it.

"After a few visits, Glenn Kirby asked us if we'd like to do an overview study of the Bible with another couple as teachers. We agreed, and that's how we met Rod and Rita. Over the next several months, as the historical panorama of God's plan was explained, the combination of the Holy Spirit's work and Rod and Rita's guidance and testimony convinced Bonny and me that we were on the right track. Before we completed the study, we asked Jesus into our lives and were baptized."

Now the cycle has been completed as the Setsers have become teachers of the overview, and their first students, the Paladinos, have also joined the church.

The actual format of each session is up to the individual teacher. Usually the people take turns reading a portion of Scripture, discuss its content, and answer the questions in the workbook.

Sometimes a student may feel lost or be very shy — and the teacher must do all the talking. Other times a student can't read well, and the teacher must do all the reading from Scripture. But most sessions are a free-flowing discussion with plenty of time for personal questions. Ideally everyone has done the workbook lesson ahead of time, allowing more time for personal application and questions. If students really want to dig into the Word, the sessions may go for several hours — and the study for several months.

Many students have in-depth theories concerning Creation, the Flood, the tower of Babel, or prophecy. We don't try to put down their theories, but we do try to teach the Scriptures simply. Some discover that their theories really don't matter — what matters is the message clearly recorded in Scripture.

But in addition to understanding Bible history, the student is developing a personal relationship with an experienced Christian. Some of these relationships are the strongest in the church.

Currently we have 33 separate studies in progress with 46 students involved, and another church is teaching this course in an adult Sunday school class. In the past year, our Sunday school has grown 15 percent.

The benefits of this ministry are many:

- More and more people gain experience teaching.
- New teachers overcome their fears because they're already familiar with the material and they simply follow the workbook.
- Teachers demonstrate Bible study methods and model the Christian life — two keys to discipleship.
- Close relationships are developed, which build a bridge to establish students in Sunday school and worship services.

But by far the most important benefit we've experienced is the excitement among our members when they see friends accept Christ. Not only does it make them want to keep teaching, but it helps the church actually do what everyone talks about — make disciples.

A Notebook for Growing

If you watch people walking into South Sheridan Baptist Church in Lakewood, Colorado, you'll notice up to a third of them carrying a 5½-by-8½ blue notebook.

A glimpse of the cover will reveal the title "Words of Wisdom," a logo, and a Scripture: "Wise men lay up knowledge. Proverbs 10:14." Inside the three-ring binder are tab dividers: (1) Sermon Notes, (2) Sunday School Notes, (3) Personal Devotions, (4) Evening Bible Study, (5) Prayer Lists, and (6) General. Printed, prepunched forms appear in the various sections.

"We put these together to help people organize their spiritual lives," explains Sparky Pritchard, associate pastor. "We sell them in the book room and the Sunday school office for $4, and they've been a real help to many."

Several have reported that the notebook has disciplined them to absorb the deeper meaning of Scripture. "We dealt with one man whose home was falling apart; he wasn't giving leadership to it, and in fact, he had separated from his wife. We gave him specific assignments to do in his personal devotions, using the notebook. Before long, he said, 'I didn't realize the Bible could be so real and could apply directly to my situation.' Today, that marriage is back together."

During sermons, listeners can be seen jotting notes in their blue binders. When prayer needs are mentioned, they update their lists.

A final benefit, says Pritchard, is that the books arouse interest among members' friends and lead to witnessing opportunites.

The Witness Stand

Hearing how God has changed the lives of people beside you in the pew is an effective way to breathe life into a church. How can that energy be included regularly in the Sunday morning service?

At the Christian and Missionary Alliance Church in Cheyenne, Wyoming, Richard Birr began prearranging to have one person each week come to "The Witness Stand" to testify how he or she became a Christian.

"We've now had over 50 people share their faith this way," says Birr. "This part of the worship service has become a highlight."

Birr says only rarely have people refused his invitation to take the stand. "Knowing they are among friends, plus some timely persuasion on my part in some instances, is usually all it takes — even for those who've never done anything like this before," says Birr. "Even the most nervous have done a beautiful job."

A Word from the Pew

One member of The Federated Church in Columbus, Nebraska, gives a personal testimony each Sunday morning — in the bulletin.

Lana Danielson, a high school English teacher, "thought it would be a bonus to have parishioners share their 'faith journeys' with the rest of the congregation," says Pastor Lee Hicks. She helped gather a six-member Meditation and Inspiration Board to solicit and edit a weekly bulletin insert. In 200-300 words a member expresses some aspect of his or her Christian walk:

● One woman told what she was learning by corresponding with a prison inmate.

- Another person probed the idea of how we hurt God at times.
- Another wrote on what Lent means and how to make the most of it.

"This has been a real source of help to our congregation," says Hicks. Some obvious advantages:

- It's a good alternative for those who are frightened by public speaking.
- It's not an overwhelming task for most people.
- The format is convenient and still gets high readership — probably more than a full-fledged parish newspaper, which is a lot more work.
- It brightens and lightens the glut of announcements in the average church bulletin.

Dads Who Mean Business

When F.A.T.H.E.R.S. get together at Cincinnati's College Hill Presbyterian Church, they do more than swap fish stories. The acronym stands for Fathers And Their Home Environment Relationships Studies — an intensive two-year course in the skills of fathering.

"I invited fathers to join me, not for inspiration, but for action," says Ron Rand, associate pastor. Twenty-seven signed up, even though it meant meeting at 6:30 every Monday morning for worship, prayer, instruction, and discussion. The group has divided into two companies — older fathers and younger ones. Each company in turn is divided into units of four called squads for mutual support and accountability. "We hold each other accountable to five basic disciplines," says Rand.

1. To pray daily for wife, children, and others.
2. To read Scripture daily according to a definite plan.
3. To participate at least weekly in the worship of God.

4. To serve others daily.

5. To study and develop a sound mind through reading Scripture and other pertinent literature.

They also keep each other honest with a calendar check. Each man has committed himself to a weekly "club-time" with each child (30 minutes of focused attention in play or a special activity) and a special date with his wife. "When you know the others are going to check up on your commitment, it's amazing how you get it done," one man observes.

Besides developing their own fathering skills, the men are committed to helping others. They publish a T.I.P. (Try It, Pop!) each month in the church newsletter. After a year of training, each man seeks another father to disciple in the same way. They are also planning creative help for the church school program.

Reported by Douglas J. Rumford

WHERE FAMILY DEVOTIONS ARE ALIVE AND WELL

by Mark R. Littleton, pastor, Berea Baptist Church, Glen Burnie, Maryland

I hadn't realized how discouraged I was until I sat in my office one October and stared into space for 10 minutes straight. "Lord, what is wrong?" I finally prayed.

Rarely has the "still, small voice" spoken so quickly and clearly. "You need to teach these people how to walk with me as *families*. What about Richard Baxter?"

Right, Richard Baxter. Just the week before I'd read how Baxter, after three years without results in an affluent English church in the 1600s, had gone from house to house teaching his people how to have family worship. You know — devotions. The thing we wrap today with gimmicks and games, and everyone still gives up.

But the voice was persistent. I'd been working with about 10 to 15 individuals, teaching them how to have a Quiet Time. Why not whole families?

To a few people I volunteered the idea of my stopping over in the morning for devotions . . . and got mostly strange looks and mumbled excuses.

"What now, Lord?"

Another heart message: "Why don't you start with the ones *I* want you to start with?"

"Right, but who?"

"Just sit tight."

The next day I stopped at a new convert's home to encourage him. A night-shift worker, he was fighting a hard battle with alcoholism. "He's down at the bar," his wife told me after I knocked at the door. "Been there since 6:30 this morning." Her son was on the way to bring him home.

When he showed up, he was crocked, but friendly. He admitted everything, too. The whole family situation was killing him.

I'd tried counseling him. I'd even written down what to do on three-by-five cards. We'd been praying for him in church. He was in a good Sunday school class. But still, here he was, smashed.

I held my breath, then asked, "What about having us meet — you, me, and your wife — for devotions every morning after you get off work till we get you dry?"

"Anything you say, pastor!" I liked that kind of response.

So we met every weekday morning at 7:30 for no-frills devotions. First, we memorized a new verse by repeating it together out loud. Then we reviewed old verses, talked about what they meant, and found some applications.

Next, we read three to five chapters of the Bible using *The Daily Walk* (from Walk Thru the Bible Ministries, which takes readers through the whole Bible in one year). After reading silently, we'd discuss the passage and look for specific applications.

Last, we prayed, writing our requests in a notebook and filling in the answers when they came.

The insights were fast, furious, and curious. I was amazed at this couple's enthusiasm. I was amazed at my enthusiasm! Most of all, we were amazed at the Lord's enthusiasm in sending so many prayer answers, insights, laughs, and tears. The husband stayed dry. We settled numerous problems that many would reserve for long-term counseling simply by talking things out on the basis of Scripture. Even their children, both non-Christian single adults, sat in occasionally. At Christmas they both presented me with beautiful gifts, telling me, "You deserve more than this for all you've done for Mom and Dad. They're getting it together." I went home and wept.

We had morning devotions together for three weeks, then went to a twice-a-week schedule. Meanwhile, other families wanted help. One had experienced some infidelity. Another had serious marital problems with actual physical abuse. A third had a runaway child. A fourth was a couple who had been "living together" and wanted to find something that lasted. Still another just wanted to know what it meant to be a Christian. Rather than proposing counseling, seminar-attending, and so on, I suggested family devotions to all.

I met some families in the morning, as early as 6:00 A.M. Others I met in the evening, after dinner or later, sometimes when the children were in bed. I have met with some as often as every weekday, with others as infrequently as once every two weeks. I began tapering off altogether with some families as they began to be able to go it alone. But I had to meet several months before they got to that point.

The first family and I did not meet at one point for two weeks because of illness. I feared they were slipping, and I called one morning at 10:30 with fear and trembling. "How are you doing? I haven't been by for a while. Have you still been studying together?"

The husband answered. "We're doing our Bible work right now. Been at it since 8:00. Frieda's whipping through all her Bibles, and we're digging it out."

"Since 8:00! What are you studying?" It had to be something absolutely riveting.

"Leviticus 25-27. You know, the reading for today."

I almost fell over. I always skipped those sections. "Yeah, but we've been going back and studying all this clean and unclean stuff. Do you know those people weren't allowed to eat crabs? And pigs? No bacon or anything!"

When I came by the next day, they told me, "We're going to start meeting with the next-door neighbors. They want to see what we're doing, because they like studying the Bible, too."

Another family wanted to start an evangelistic devotional study for several friends whose lives were falling apart. I suggested we do the Book of Revelation (you know, a little sensationalism to hook them). They said, "Well, that's OK, but we'd rather start in Genesis and go right through the Bible. You think we could do that on Tuesday nights?" This from a couple who were railing against the church six months ago as a bunch of money grubbers.

A third family with whom I met at 6:00 A.M. commented, "Everybody keeps telling us how much we've changed. We aren't even fighting anymore."

Many mornings I stumbled to their door at 6:05 or so, bleary-eyed and bushed, awakened them, and began the devotions with them still in their pajamas. One moaned about a headache, another about all the lost sleep because the baby kept waking up. But after we'd be going for an hour, the husband would comment, "You know what? My headache's gone. This is really a good way to start the day." The wife would say, "Yeah, I don't even feel like going back to bed now."

Obviously, it's hard to wake up at 5:30 day after day, drag myself out, and put on a devotional face. Sometimes I take *long* naps during the day. But one thing is for sure: When people say things like "You're the greatest pastor I've ever had" and "I never knew walking with God could be so good," I know I can't quit. Showing families how to meet God through his Word and prayer is just about the most practical thing a pastor can do.

A Big Push
for Small Groups

Any church that's ever tried to start home fellowship groups has found that while some members are eager, others conveniently ignore the groups. Sharing with a few fellow Christians can be more threatening than it sounds.

When The Church on the Way in Van Nuys, California, launched groups back in 1977, they made them supremely obvious: they canceled two Sunday morning services in deference to the home meetings. Once in August and again in September, there was no worship in the sanctuary — "your only option was to go to your home group," says Dennis Corrigan, director of discipleship and small-group ministry.

"Then at the beginning of 1978, we asked one-fourth of our groups to meet on each Sunday morning of the month. The congregation was growing dramatically at that point, and this had the pleasant by-product of relieving our space squeeze by one-fourth. But that was not the main point: what we wanted was to impress people with the importance of house-to-house fellowship."

Now that a larger building has been completed, yet another schedule has been instituted. The first Sunday night of each month is "Rainbow Night" — the normal evening service is canceled, and groups meet in homes. Groups also meet later in the month for a social occasion on whatever date they choose.

"We do, however, hold a small first-Sunday-night service at the church for drop-ins," Corrigan adds. "In fact, that has turned out to be a fairly effective evangelistic opportunity. Those who show up not knowing it's our small-group night are often the ones seeking spiritual help."

Home Bible Studies:
What to Do with the Kids

Many churches are enthusiastic about cell group meetings in homes, but parents with younger children face a crunch: Shall they hire a babysitter, or shall they bring their kids along and hope they behave during the adult interaction? Here's how two groups are dealing with the problem.

In Durango, Colorado, Sam Holt's small group has a special family night once a month. Each family presents a project — a skit, a song, a puppet show — to the other five families in the group. The continuing Bible study is laid aside this evening in favor of the six presentations.

"This not only includes the children in our group," says Holt, pastor of First Baptist Church, "but it also gives a focus to family worship throughout the month.

"I'd tried several other approaches to home devotions that failed, and I was asking myself, 'What can I do to get families moving in this area?' The monthly project has finally brought results, because it has accountability tied to it. Parents teach biblical truths at home in the process of preparing something to present to the rest of the group.

"Actually, the kids are the ones who pull the grownups along. They love getting ready; my own young children are constantly pushing me: 'Let's make up another puppet show for the Bible study.'"

Holt tells about one family who arrived unprepared one month. "Even that became a learning experience," he says. "They began analyzing what had hindered them in the preceding days — was it busyness, too much TV, fatigue, or what?"

On the other three Wednesday nights of the month, the group's children stay at home with babysitters.

The Chinese Alliance Church's study group in Wheaton, Illinois, brings its children each Friday night and entertains them with a children's videocassette, a hired teenager, and popcorn.

"Our children range from infants to seven-year-olds," says Pastor David Wong, "and we tried having some very creative people teach the children while the adults had their Bible study. But no one seemed to be willing to stick with this ministry; they either ran out of creative ideas or patience.

"One night we met in a home that had a video player. We rented a children's movie, and our problem was suddenly solved.

"So far we've used Walt Disney films, cartoons, and some Warner Brothers features. Our town library rents videocassettes for as low as $2 a day, and video stores aren't much higher. Meanwhile, the teenager has a stand ing job for every Friday evening."

HONING THE TWO-EDGED SWORD

by D. Paul Stevens, teaching elder, Marineview Chapel,
Vancouver, British Columbia

Disobedience to God's Word needs no encouragement;
it's abundant enough, thank you. Yet without intending to, local churches frequently establish patterns that hinder actually *doing* the Word.

The formula is deceptively simple: Expose people to
more biblical material than they can digest, do it in a context
separated from real life, and emphasize Bible facts, not personal acts.

Imagine the typical situation of a new believer: He
attends a Sunday morning Bible class studying Paul's three
missionary journeys. Full of excitement from Dr. Luke's dy-
namic account of worldwide salvation in Jesus (but with no
time to assimilate it), he enters the sanctuary for worship.
The sermon is "Speaking Covenant: The Ultimate Language
of Love," part of a series on Hosea. The new believer is impressed with the need for covenant love in both his relationship with God and with his spouse.

On the way out, he picks up the current copy of *Daily
Light*. Using this or some other excellent plan for daily Bible
study, he'll spend six brief sessions in Psalms.

If he's really serious, he'll also attend a midweek Bible
study/prayer group, where the parables are being taught. But
they won't explode in his mind either, because he's still half-
thinking about what the TV evangelist said last night.

He's effectively been inoculated.

In the Great Commission, Jesus calls not for teaching the Word but "teaching them to obey" (Matt. 28:20). *Doing,* not *hearing* biblical truth is the measure of biblical faith. When we encourage gathering information or even inspiration without learning to live it, we unwittingly encourage disobedience. We erect barriers against the Holy Spirit.

Kierkegaard once said, "The moment I take Christianity as a doctrine and so indulge my cleverness or profundity or eloquence or imaginative powers in depicting it, people are very pleased; I am looked upon as a serious Christian. The moment I begin to express existentially what I say, and consequently bring Christianity into reality, it is just as though I had exploded existence — the scandal is there at once" (*Journals, 343*).

In an effort to bring Christianity into reality, I began twenty years ago to explore the concept of an integrated congregational curriculum.

I was pastoring Temple Baptist Church in inner-city Montreal, a multicultural fellowship where I was challenged to communicate God's Word to five diverse ethnic groups.

We wrote a lectionary of daily readings that led us systematically through whole books of the Bible. During the week, our neighborhood meetings in homes of church members would discuss three or four simple questions we had mimeographed to help them apply the readings of the week. Then on Sunday I preached from the study portion assigned for that week. The community walked with me through a passage they'd already studied.

From that experience I learned the principle of *reinforced learning:* People are more likely to "do the doctrine" when they meet that same word in more than one environment.

Ten years later, at West Point Grey Baptist Church in Vancouver, British Columbia, the integrated approach took a quantum leap forward. I discovered that a lasting lesson is learned when people find it for themselves.

"Standing at the bus stop the other day," one of the older sisters confessed to me, "I tried to remember something from all the sermons I've heard over 30 years. My mind went totally blank. But I was flooded with gratitude when I recalled the things I'd discovered for myself in the Scriptures."

We designed a curriculum that aimed at learning rather than teaching. We'd spend eleven weeks, for instance, in Ephesians. Besides the daily Bible readings, we would offer a weekly personal Bible study section and a group experience.

The personal study was a series of inductive questions. Each person would *observe* (what does it say?), *interpret* (what does it mean?), and *apply* (what does it mean to me?). The notes we provided gave a minimum of information — only what was needed to make sense of the text.

The group study each week took the same passage and applied it to corporate life. Discussion questions helped the groups make fresh discoveries as needs, gifts, and concerns surfaced from exposure to the Word. An optional group relational exercise attempted to apply the Scripture to relationships within the group. Relationships, we found, are not only an area of application but of illumination.

For example, after studying 1 Corinthians 12 and Romans 12, one group genuinely experienced the truth that "the parts of the body which seem to be weaker are indispensable, and those . . . we think less honorable we invest with the greater honor." They spent an entire evening focusing on one person at a time and answering the question "How has this person been used by God to minister to this group or to individuals?" They were amazed to find out how many ways the seemingly awkward personalities had been essential to the health of the group.

The small groups became examples of faith on display, living demonstrations of biblical truth.

What a privilege on Sunday to teach people who had read the passage, discussed it among themselves, and encountered it corporately. Not once in 20 years has anyone complained of repetition of the same text. The most common criticism has been that we were moving too quickly through the Scripture.

Often the Sunday sermon was based on something that surfaced in our Tuesday small group. No longer the lonely prophet descending from the mountain to deliver the Sunday message, I was now a fellow learner in the camp, sharing what God was teaching us all. We learned the meaning of 1 John 2:27 — "You do not need anyone to teach you." It doesn't mean teaching elders are unnecessary. Far from threatening my position, it actually enhanced it through a corporate anointing of the Spirit.

Thus at West Point Grey, I learned the principle of *discovery learning:* People will integrate into their lives what they've discovered for themselves.

Now here at Marineview Chapel in Vancouver, I've divested myself of an additional clerical prerogative: I no longer write the curriculum myself. A group of eight or nine, selected by the elders, meet to discuss the upcoming texts, identifying the major themes we need to confront, and then divide up the writing assignments. They meet again to critique one another's work before one of the elders edits and takes the material to the printer. Thus, our curricula are fully homegrown, uniquely aimed, and rarely suitable for other congregations without radical editing.

Each year the elders select the learning plan, which includes at least one Old Testament book, one New Testament book, and a contemporary topic such as economic lifestyle, spiritual formation, public discipleship, or something current in the pilgrimage of our church.

We plan one- or two- week gaps between series to give people a break from the daily readings, give the groups a chance to do something other than Bible study, and allow the elders to preach in response to some immediate need. This helps us avoid overprogramming and allows us to scratch where people are itching.

For instance, when a group at Marineview got excited about radical community, the elders, instead of ignoring them as a threatening irritation, welcomed this as a learning moment. We were in the midst of trying to decide whether to spend $3 million for a bigger building or reorganize some-how to make do with what we had. The group was invited to prepare a topical study for the whole church to investigate scriptural principles of congregational life. The eight-week se-ries helped shape our eventual decision to divide the con-gregation into three working communities, each with its own meeting time on Sunday, its own cluster of elders, and its own network of house groups. Not only were we better able to handle 600 people in our small building, but fresh leadership and new gifts emerged.

Occasionally we provide a section of family studies for parents to use with their children, which has been moderately successful. But simply by helping parents become biblically literate, we're equipping them to become better educators of their children.

This then is the principle of *equipping through Bible learn-ing*. Whatever I can do to help people become competent in ministry is more valuable to the body than any ministry I can perform directly, no matter how excellent.

We've enjoyed several advantages of this pattern of ministry.

● It encourages obedience, not disobedience. Discovery learning helps people *do* doctrine by focusing on one passage at a time at multiple levels: personal Bible study, group dis-cussions, congregational life, and the preached Word. And yet over time, people are exposed to "the whole counsel of God," not just the preacher's pet portions.

● It helps unify the body. Often pastors fear that small groups will lead to schism or independent fragments within the body. We've found, however, that when all the groups study the same Scripture, we are unified through the Word during the week and the Sacrament on Sunday.

● It breeds spiritual health. More people do personal Bible study, which means Sunday is no longer their only spiri-tual lifeline. Our group studies often begin with "What did you learn in your personal study this week?" It encourages accountability.

● It makes the pastor or teaching elder an equipper. By developing a congregational curriculum, the Christian worker becomes a theological and biblical resource person rather than a solo entertainer. It helps give the ministry away without giving it up.

Columnist Russell Baker once wrote that "the number of places where a person can escape entertainment becomes smaller every year." Sadly, the church is also a victim of this social conformity. But when pulpit and pew work together through a common curriculum to obey the Word of God, we help create a more natural environment to grow into maturity.

That's a lot better than becoming inoculated by small doses of scattered but pleasing religious entertainment.

HOW TO WRITE BIBLE-STUDY MATERIAL

Marineview Chapel provides three pages of tips for those who write study guides, including these suggestions:

Personal Study Sections

Vary the level on which you appeal. For example, some questions may require reflection and continuing study. In this case, you should occasionally say, "If you are unable to answer this question now, come back to it later." Other questions could be multiple choice questions or selecting a number on a scale of responses. (This is especially good for suggested applications.) Occasionally use a chart with fill-in sections.

Avoid routine, liturgical exhortations such as starting *ev-ry* study with "Pray for the leading of the Holy Spirit." But do intersperse encouragements such as "Stop for a moment to ask God to show you how this fits into your life."

Test your study by doing it yourself. Time it. (It shouldn't be more than an hour.) Then ask someone who has never studied the passage to do it and tell you what questions were vague or irrelevant.

Sometimes it's valuable to "tease" more advanced students by suggesting an optional exercise: a hard interpretive question, a word study, or if you're in the Old Testament, a parallel New Testament passage.

Avoid yes/no questions and those with too obvious answers. But avoid overchallenging and thus discouraging beginning learners.

Resist the temptation to "rig the truth" so that people make *your* discovery. Questions shouldn't leave people asking, "What was the writer driving at?" Instead, help people make fresh discoveries for themselves.

Make sure every personal study leads to some actions to "do the doctrine."

Group Study Materials

Assume that everyone is doing personal study. Build into the group study at least one specific contribution from personal study. Here are some ideas:

Divide the passage into sections and have each member share in one minute what he or she learned from that section. This will need to be set up the previous week, but this way the whole passage is surveyed briefly and everyone shares.

Build into the personal study a specific point that will be shared with the group, such as "The one prayer request I have for this group as as result of studying this passage is . . ."

Ask one member in advance to teach the passage in 10-15 minutes at the beginning of the meeting.

Group Relational Exercises

These focus on applying the passage to our relationships as a group. Particular passages may suggest exercises in the following areas:

— affirming one another's gifts
— communicating our feelings, experiences
— developing a Christian concept of leadership, order, servanthood, plurality, inner authority, and freedom.

In writing relational exercises, some guidelines need to be spelled out, using such statements as "Make sure everyone shares his viewpoint on this," "Limit this part of the discussion to 20 minutes," "No one is allowed to communicate a negative thing while we are affirming strengths," and "Make sure no one's prayer request is ignored; write them all down."

The Day a Chain Saw Came to Church

Living the Christian life is a seven-day-a-week occupation, but how can a once-a-week Sunday school class reinforce that?

At Chestnut Street Baptist Church in Ellensburg, Washington, James Powell's unique idea not only helps people focus on living their faith during the week, but it also has:

- livened up the adult Sunday school program,
- given incentive for people to arrive on time,
- acquainted them with what fellow class members do for a living.

Dr. Powell, adult Sunday school director, gathers all the adult classes together for a 15-minute opening session each Sunday. Each week a different person presents the tools of his or her trade and a spiritual truth they illustrate.

One Sunday logger Paul Maurer demonstrated the use of his chain saw and double-bitted axe. Emphasis: sharp tools work most effectively. Truth: God's Word is sharper than a two-edged sword (or a double-bitted axe!)

Another week a violinist played three pieces — a beginning piece, an intermediate number, and an advanced score. Emphasis: becoming skilled requires practice. Truth: to become skilled in handling Scripture, Christians must practice by continually reading and studying the Bible.

Yet another time, a doctor showed how to use surgical tools. Emphasis: every profession has a set of tools. Truth: a Christian's tools are prayer and God's Word.

"Not only does this give adults a chance to be in a teaching role," says Powell, "but it also provides real-life illustrations of spiritual truths."

Powell meets with the speaker beforehand to think

through the possible applications and the aspect of the job that best illustrates the truth.

The talks have caught the imagination of the classes.

"A number of adults and college students have suggested new ideas or volunteered themselves for future demonstrations," says Powell.

Perhaps the most benefit goes to the speakers. Bringing their jobs to church usually means they'll take their Christian application back to work on Monday.
Reported by Deborah Dunn

HELPING CHRISTIANS GO TO WORK

by Donald Patterson, pastor, First Presbyterian Church, Jackson, Mississippi

Editor's note: More than one layman has said (or at least thought), "Why is it my church deals with almost every aspect of my life except my employment? My devotional life, my family, my marriage, my service in the church — everything gets emphasized but what I do eight to ten hours a day."

In the following article, a pastor describes his church's attempt to speak to people occupationally. His case deals with the medical community, but other churches may well consider similar events for sales and marketing people, teachers, farmers, construction workers, or almost any group.

Our church lies within a mile of five hospitals, so we have always had a generous supply of professional people. For a long time I wondered if we could somehow help equip these men and women to practice medicine in a Christlike manner. Could physicians, dentists, and nurses reach their colleagues better than I could? It made sense to me, but I had no model to follow and not much encouragement.

At times I asked similar questions about the lawyers who were part of First Presbyterian. How could we guide them to apply their faith in their unique positions of influence?

Then, in June, 1980, I attended the Consultation on World Evangelization in Thailand, where the main emphasis was on reaching people by ethnic group. I came home more convinced than ever that we all do best at reaching others like ourselves.

About this time, John Tanksley, a senior medical student, came by my study with a problem. The philosophy of teaching at the University of Mississippi Medical School, he reported, was thoroughly humanistic. Nothing in his courses seemed to relate to the Christian physician and his family life, ethics, or finances. His question still rings in my ears: "Can't we rub shoulders with some of your Christian doctors and get some help?"

Out of that conversation was born a conference entitled "Christ and the Healing Arts." A joint committee of church members and persons from the Christian Medical Fellowship on the campus began to ask some hard questions:

● "Why do we begin our careers with compassion for people, only to grow cold and hardened and concerned with the pursuit of more money?"

● "Why do we allow professional status to obsess us more than patient care?"

● "What's happened to our feeling of excitement about helping people?"

● "Why do we relax academic discipline as we grow more and more independent?"

The weekend conference that November featured Stephen F. Olford, radio voice of Encounter Ministries, and six practicing physicians and dentists who shared about the grace of God in their lives. More than 300 medical personnel attended. At the close of the Sunday morning service, more than 50 responded to an invitation to yield everything to Jesus Christ.

As we totaled up the cost of the event, we realized for less than $1,000 we had made a sizable impact on the medical community of central Mississippi. Three weekly Bible studies were started in the dental school, and the Christian Medical Fellowship noted a significant increase in interest.

The committee re-formed itself under the authority of the church's session and began planning immediately for the fall of 1981. Frank Barker, pastor of Briarwood Presbyterian Chruch in Birmingham, Alabama, was asked to be the key-noter, but he could only come on the weekend of the Ole Miss — Mississippi State football game, the biggest grudge match of the year.

John Tanksley, William Harper, and the rest of the committee decided to "turn lemon into lemonade." They rearranged the schedule a bit to avoid conflict with the festivities. Barker was asked to bring gifted physicians and dentists from Birmingham. Excitement was high on Friday evening when approximately 700 medical people from all over the state of Mississippi attended the service.

Seminars the next morning dealt with issues such as abortion, death, finances, and ethics. A workshop for doctor's wives was included, along with a session on overseas ministry options. Medical students were able to interact with some of the finest internists and cardiologists in the Southeast. Dental students were challenged to share their faith. On Sunday morning, the sanctuary was crowded for both services, and again professional men and women were moved to consider God's claims upon their lives.

Expenses ran higher in 1981, exceeding our budget. A football weekend proved to be tough competition. But God worked, and lives were changed. Both the medical school and the dental school have a strong Christian witness today as a direct result of these conferences. People have been exposed to a Christian world and life view. Some faced the matter of abortion more seriously than ever before. Many Christians were encouraged to realize they aren't alone in their field.

What would I like to see in the future? A similar conference for attorneys. Jackson, being the state capital, has a large concentration of lawyers. With little or no application of Christian principles in their training, it doesn't surprise me that even the Christian attorney finds it difficult to practice law Christianly. Why not a conference to deal with that issue?

Occupations are where we all spend a major portion of our waking hours. Our church is excited to be reaching out to people from this perspective.

A Start Worth Honoring

Like many congregations, Glenfield Baptist Church in Glen Ellyn, Illinois, has a remembrance plaque to honor its sons and daughters who have become pastors, missionaries, or other full-time ministers.

"But by the time formal preparation is concluded and a person is launched into a field of service, " says Pastor Donnie Whitney, "years have passed, and the home church may forget its connection with the person."

So Glenfield has an additional category on its plaque: "Those Formally Recommended to Seminary" (a requirement to enroll at Southern Baptist institutions). An engraved name plate is added for each student who begins the trail toward ordination.

"We don't want to forget anyone whose ministry has its roots here," says Whitney. "This method keeps the name before us from the time they leave."

Worship Away from Home

If you're trying to encourage worship attendance, summer is surely the wrong time to launch a promotion. Right?

Wrong. First Baptist Church in Batesburg, South Carolina, discovered a subtle and unselfish way to give worship a boost.

"With summer just around the corner, we were dreading the drop in worship attendance and offerings that was as certain as the summer heat," says Pastor Marion D. Aldridge. "But trying to promote our own worship services seemed a bit egotistical. How do you ask people to come for great preaching and singing without sounding awkward or arrogant?"

Figuring that other churches felt the same bind,

First Baptist decided to encourage its vacationing members to attend other churches. The method was simple. A bulletin board was placed in the foyer displaying a large map of the United States (available from an automobile club).

"We asked people to bring us bulletins from the churches they attended while on vacation," says Aldridge. "Or they could mail us a postcard. We encouraged them to report business trips, too."

Colored pins identified towns where members visited.

"If somebody traveled west or north, we put in a pin for all of their significant sightseeing stops," says Aldridge. As people returned postcards or bulletins from other churches, they were tacked up around the map, a visual reminder that people throughout the country are worshiping God.

But Aldridge didn't stop there.

"We planned a worship service in the early fall during which our members could give vacation testimonies about their worship experiences in different places that summer."

From the floor of the sanctuary, Aldridge asked questions to spark the sharing.

"How many of you worshiped in Baptist churches this summer? What other denominations?"

"How many worshiped in larger churches? How many in smaller churches?"

"How many worshiped in more formal churches? Less formal?"

"Then I asked particular individuals what difference they noticed in forms of worship," says Aldridge. "The people got so wrapped up in the sharing time that I never got a chance to tell about *my* vacation worship experiences.

"By the way, our attendance and offerings that summer stayed up better than ever before. By going to church while on vacation, people didn't have a chance to get out of the habit. So we ended up promoting worship in our church after all!"

WHERE THE DIVORCED GET MORE THAN SYMPATHY

by John J. van der Graaf, pastor, St. Mark's United Methodist Church, Florissant, Missouri

Not often does a specialty group in a church soar to 200 members in its first year. The key here was neither spectacular programming nor high-powered promotion. Our only explanation is that we touched a population segment that was hurting.

Late one July afternoon in 1981, as another recently divorced woman left my office wiping her tears, it struck me that people like her really had no place of their own, particularly in church. They didn't fit in single's groups comprised mainly of young adults never married. They didn't feel fully accepted in the church's family activities. In the one place people come to seek support and solace, divorced people continued to feel lonely, rejected, and forgotten.

I made a resolution to see what St. Mark's could do to meet their special needs. First, I asked a divorcée named Norma Smith for ideas. We began to map out a ministry to separated and divorced people in our community.

As we talked about starting a support group, we knew what we did *not* want. We were not interested in simply a place for socializing, for "date-hunters," or for "painalogues" — the tiresome routine of "Let me tell how rotten MY husband/wife was to me!" It must be, we determined, a group that provided education, emotional, and psychological support, and spiritual affirmation and nurture. That called for definite structure.

We were clear from the beginning that we did not condone divorce. In fact, we hated it. Because we knew the hurt and pain it causes, we wanted to reach out in love and enable such people to begin life anew.

Which should come first — acceptance and caring or correction and the call to repentance for past wrongs? I'm a firm believer that people have to take responsibility for their own behavior, and I knew from my counseling that hard questions had to be faced somewhere along the way. What caused the marriage to fail? Since the majority of divorced people do remarry eventually, it was all the more important that they learn from past failures, admit wrongs, and prepare for a healthy relationship in the future.

But that was not the starting point, we decided. First we had to try to bind up the wounds.

Following our discussion, Norma and I hand-picked five divorced persons to meet and evaluate our thoughts and ideas. That group enthusiastically decided to form "Divorced Christians of North County" (our church is located in north St. Louis County).

At further weekly meetings, this steering committee outlined nine monthly meetings. Topics included:

- The Biblical and Theological Approaches to Divorce
- Feelings in Divorce
- Re-entry into Society
- Financial Management
- Self-Image and Self-Esteem
- Children, Custody, and Guilt Feelings
- Remarriage: Legal and Emotional Ramifications

I recruited a psychotherapist, a financial counselor, and an attorney for some of the topics, accepting others for myself.

Our first meeting was set for September 1, 1981. We sent letters to all the United Methodist churches in our area and also placed notices in neighborhood newspapers.

Fifteen people showed up.

News of the group spread, and it began to grow rapidly. We quickly realized that once a month would not be enough. We decided to meet each Thursday evening from 7 to 9:30. People from throughout the north county suburban area and from every denomination began to attend.

The 2½-hour format has remained constant:

1. A half hour of socializing over coffee
2. Presentation by the evening's speaker
3. Small-group discussion of the presentation
4. Open discussion in plenary session
5. Group business and adjournment

Name tags, of course, are a must in this kind of meeting. So is child care.

A governing council was elected from within the membership. Through the help of Elaine Pusczek, a member of the group, we found Paul Johnson, a United Methodist minister who, divorced himself and experienced in working with such programs, is now a therapist and divorce/marriage mediator. We contracted with Paul to be the group's ongoing facilitator. Another pastor, Harry Smith, helped us get financial support from the denomination's St. Louis North District and from other churches and sources. The name was then changed to the "North District Divorced/Separated Group."

Paul Johnson describes it as "a place where all can experience the warmth, strength, and healing of love and acceptance. With it comes faith and hope that there is life, abundant and whole, after divorce. It is a joy to be a part of this program and to share with these people."

The leadership within the group itself is remarkable. All these people needed was a sense that the church cared about them and would support them. They took over the organizational tasks and responsibilities and have carried them with enthusiasm, creativity, and diligence. They have their own fund raisers, social events (though these are of low priority), and service projects.

In the small groups that follow each evening's presentation, the discussion is honest and direct. Members can be quite confrontive at times, pointing out the problems that led to divorce and urging one another to change. They see this as part of their function. But they always speak in love, never browbeating, always showing a better way.

The support of St. Mark's 1,300 members has come from the belief that our ministry is to share acceptance and forgiveness with all people. We do not believe God has taken a vacation and appointed us to be judges in his absence. We do believe he has appointed us to be the channels of his love. In a suburban community where many, many families have been touched by divorce, this was the only reasonable response.

By forming and supporting this group, St. Mark's has become the home church for many who were previously unchurched. By 1983, a network of three such groups had spanned metropolitan St. Louis. Two of the groups meet in United Methodist churches, one in an Episcopal church. Our group is also starting a similar ministry in the central Missouri community of Moberly. One of our St. Mark's members is a pilot who regularly flies members there to provide help and organizational expertise.

Jesus said, "Go and sin no more." He also said, "You must be born again." Through our ministry to the divorced and separated, we are helping both of these commandments to become a reality in the lives of lonely, rejected, and forgotten people.

PRAYER

Sharing That Edifies

"Sharing time" (otherwise known as "prayer request time" or "testimony time") can be the best or the worst part of a service, depending on what's shared.

At Northwest Baptist Church in Chicago, sharing is encouraged on Sunday morning, with microphones in the aisles for persons to use. The following guidelines appear in the bulletin periodically to nudge participants in the right direction:

1. *When sharing a matter, be as* brief *as possible. Let us know just as much as we need to know to intelligently join you in prayer. A lot of details or an extended report of conversation are not the best use of our limited time.*

2. *Please refrain from referring to anyone along denominational, ethnic, or racial lines. Those kinds of references could be easily misunderstood.*

3. *Matters of an extremely delicate nature might best be shared in a small group or in personal one-to-one relationship.*

4. *Strive for a balance between requests and expressions of praise and between physical/spiritual needs.*

5. *If you have a matter to share but are reluctant to do so publicly yourself, please feel free to write your request on the back of a registration card and give it to Pastor Lee before the service begins.*

6. *Don't allow our concern for items 1-3 above keep you from sharing your concerns on Sunday morning.*

"Very often this sharing time is as meaningful as the sermon itself," reports Gordon Stromberg, a board member. "The level of openness has increased gradually as trust has grown in the last two years.

"One morning the parents of a four-month-old who had died suddenly in his crib stood to ask for prayer. On another morning, a deacon's wife brought us all up short by admitting, 'I'm an alcoholic, and I need help. Please pray for me.' "

Following the sharing time, a member (asked in advance) leads in prayer for the shared items and other church needs. Quiet organ music then allows for silent intercession before the pastoral prayer.

Secret Intercessors

When Earl D. Owen came to Grace United Methodist Church in Bremen, Indiana, a dozen years ago, his idea for prayer partners hardly sounded spectacular. He simply held a Prayer Covenant Service in January at which people could, if they wished, sign a slip of paper. The two options read:

☐ *I promise to pray daily for my prayer partner.*
☐ *I wish to be prayed for daily.*

Members could check one or both statements and fill in their name, address, birthday, and anniversary.

"All we did was invite people to draw out a slip if they wished," says Owen. "Some thought this really wouldn't amount to much."

But what happened was more auspicious than any secret pal scheme, as people began quickly praying for the names they had drawn. "At the end of the year, we took an entire service to reveal our prayer partners," the pastor remembers. "The results were amazing. People told of difficult times when they *knew* someone was praying for them. Others told how a card had arrived at a critical moment, signed only by 'your prayer partner.'

"Some admitted that at first, when they had drawn the name, they hadn't even known the person. So they had set out to discover just who this was and what they were like in order to pray more intelligently."

The program has continued every year since. On

special occasions such as Easter or Christmas, the altar is filled with flowers, gifts, and cards from secret partners. "We have become a more caring fellowship of believers," says Owen.

Who Will Pray?

The members of St. Hedwig Catholic Church in Milwaukee, Wisconsin, were handed a new kind of pledge card one fall. It said not a word about money. Instead of asking "How much will you give?" the question was "How much will you pray?" Worshipers were asked to fill out a detachable portion and drop it in the collection plate.

"We received about a hundred pledges from people making personal commitments to several weeks of prayer and sharing in small groups," says Rosemary Badger, director of programs at St. Hedwig. The prayer commitment was part of an effort at spiritual renewal in the parish.

At the top of the form was the Scripture verse "Again I tell you, if two of you join your voices on Earth to pray for anything whatsoever, it shall be granted you by my Father in Heaven" (Matt. 18:19). Next came several options to check:

- Participation in Tuesday morning group prayer, 8:30 A.M.
- Participation in Thursday evening group prayer, 5:00 P.M.
- Observing one day of prayer and fasting each week
- Praying for the Scripture lessons given at Sunday Mass
- Reading and praying over Scripture for 15 minutes each day
- Special daily family prayer

"Our people suddenly felt as if they'd had a new opportunity to *feel* their faith in a real sense," Badger adds. "I think many of them had up to that point felt bound into an institution instead of into faith in Jesus."

People prayed for their friends and relatives, and they expected answers; each small group fostered a spirit of trust among the participants. "Prayers went up for those we thought had in some ways been alienated by the church," says Badger. "We prayed that they would become part of the living body of Christ again."

One woman prayed that her nephew would become a Christian; the Lord answered her prayer. An elderly person said, "Here I am, aged, but I feel like a new person again."

"It opened people up to the Holy Spirit," Badger adds, and evidently this experience has spread throughout the parish. In a local newspaper article, Ronald Crewe, pastor, wrote: "It is little wonder to me that when people have been sharing their concerns in intercessory prayer, and have gotten to know each other better in their small groups, they will find a new experience when they pray as an assembly in church."

A Tracking System for Prayer Requests

How can a pastor find out — and then conscientiously pray — about the many personal needs in a congregation? Likewise, how can people convey their hurts and requests to their pastor conveniently?

At the Church of the Nazarene in the small Michigan town of Durand, the communication happens smoothly and regularly through a three-by-five card in the pew racks. "Dear Pastor Potter," it says, "please be my prayer partner and pray with me for — " At the bottom are lines for the name, address, phone number, and date.

"People hand them to me as they leave a service, mail them to me, or deposit them in a locked box in the foyer, for which I have the only key," the pastor explains. "These cards provide me with a ready-made prayer list for the times when I go to my knees on behalf of my people.

"If a card indicates something urgent, of course I make a phone call or a visit right away. These cards have opened doors of ministry for me that otherwise would not have come."

On Sunday morning, Potter sometimes places several cards on the altar at the time of the pastoral prayer. "We promote the idea of being partners in prayer on a regular basis," he says. "Sometimes I will explain the cards in a service and have the ushers pass them out. Cards are always available beside the drop box in the foyer as well. I carry a supply with me for distributing during pastoral calls or other contacts. We've sort of become known in the community as the church with the prayer emphasis."

A direct result of this has been the formation of prayer groups.

One church member said, "The card makes me conscious that I'm not alone in my need." Another commented, "Having to put my request into words has helped me get specific about what I really want."

Best of all are the times, however, when members tell in a service of answers to prayer. Pastor Potter, having been intimately involved in the praying, is fully aware of who has exciting news to share.

Reported by C. Neil Strait

Prayer: The Proof Is in the Doing

Sometimes people find prayer a burden.

At St. Simon's Episcopal Church in Arlington Heights, Illinois, one member recently complained that the printed prayer list was getting too long. How could he pray for people he didn't know? Were prayers like that any good?

Curate John Throop wanted to demonstrate the importance of intercessory prayer and show that even when the needs are overwhelming, God isn't overwhelmed. He decided to be a model intercessor himself.

"Each day of the year I set aside a different family or single person in the church," says Throop. "I remember them in my devotions several times during their day. I also write a personal letter to each family, letting them know I'm praying for them and asking them to pray for me, too."

The results, according to Throop, "have been nothing short of amazing! On several occasions, I dropped the letter in the mail only to receive a call from that very family expressing a need, and they hadn't yet received the note. Other times people have said, 'Your letter came at just the right time — we needed those prayers,' and 'I'm so glad you care — and of course I'll pray for you.'

"I feel stronger and more cared for as a pastor. This prayer ministry is truly mutual."

Throop sees this as the necessary first step in showing the congregation that prayer is a boon, not a burden. "People need to know they're being prayed for," he says. "How can they know how to pray for others if the pastor doesn't set a clear example?"

The Prayer Connection

When was the last time someone asked, "Could I pray with you about anything in particular?"

Dale Keller, pastor of the Free Methodist church in Mattoon, Illinois, does it twice a week, every week, to stay in touch with his members' needs. "One of the priorities I have set for myself," he writes in a standard note to parishioners, "is to regularly pray for all those who regularly attend our church. . . . Please take a few moments now to jot down some of your requests so that when I call, you will be prepared. . . . I look forward to speaking and praying with you next week!"

The notes go out on Thursday, and the pastor makes his two phone calls the following Monday evening. By this regular system, he works through the entire congregation about three times a year. The two needs each week receive daily attention during Keller's personal prayer time.

"Most people manage to be home since they know I'm going to call," he says, "or else they'll hand me their request on Sunday. Naturally, some fail to think ahead, but the majority are ready when the phone rings.

"And in some cases, the timing has been almost uncanny." One family had just suffered the loss of a relative. "They were on the periphery of our church, and so they hadn't felt free to let me know. I 'happened' to call in the midst of their grieving. Suddenly I had the chance to pray with them and comfort them, and I attended the funeral as well."

Pray Now, Pray Later

Sunday school classes can sometimes be long on prayer requests and short on faithfully praying. Largo (Florida) Church of the Nazarene makes sure the requests are prayed for right away, and also has a unique way of reminding people to continue praying.

During the pastoral prayer each Sunday, worshipers are invited to come to the altar to pray for special requests. Pastor Earle Hollett also specifically invites people who've promised to pray for someone else's request.

"I remind them that they may forget their promise," says Hollett. "Here's an opportunity to make sure they remember the person who's asked them to pray."

Each Sunday 12 to 30 people will kneel at the altar.

But the concern for prayer doesn't stop on Sunday morning. Members also use a "carry out" service for requests.

In each Sunday school class, FBI cards (Faith's Bureau of Intercession) are distributed. These three-by-five cards have printed spaces where "The 10 Most Wanted" prayer requests can be written down.

Members can jot down requests and tuck them into a billfold or purse as a constant reminder.

"Once a month in the midweek service, we have a sharing time when we go over the answered requests from the cards," says Hollett.

"In the past nine months, our attendance has grown 31 percent, and we've experienced the best revival in the church's history," the pastor says. "All the credit goes to the new prayer emphasis."

Welding Stronger Prayer Chains

For as often as prayer chains seem to break, maybe they should be called prayer threads instead. "One lady in another parish told me she had been on a prayer chain for three years and had never been called," says

Bob Heublein, director of Christian education at St. Peter Lutheran Church in Schaumburg, Illinois.

Two solutions in use at St. Peter are:

- Chain members are instructed to *keep going* down the list until they reach someone, so the prayer request keeps moving. They can always go back at a later time and fill in those who weren't home initially. "This overcomes the single most frequent cause of breakdown — when the next person in your chain happens to be unavailable," says Heublein.

- Karen Crowe, the prayer chain coordinator, is diligent to put through prayers of thanksgiving for answers to earlier needs. Chain members thus hear about the results of their praying and are encouraged to continue.

Remembering to Pray

How do Christians become open enough to mention their *own* needs for prayer, not just other people's?

And how can a group remember to pray for such needs more than once?

While serving his internship at Pleasantdale Covenant Church, Troy, New York, seminarian Dick Rasanen began bringing a small basket to the midweek service. Each week he handed out pieces of paper and invited each person to write a request about themselves. Names were not required, but three-fourths of the people signed them anyway.

At the close of the meeting, each person reached into the prayer basket and took a slip of paper to pray about during the coming week.

"The benefit was twofold," says Rasanen. "We all went home confident that someone had our request and would be praying for us. Meanwhile, we all felt the need to be more disciplined in our own prayer lives, since someone was counting on us."

The following week, Rasanen would invite comments and reports on what had happened. Some openly apologized for the times they had forgotten the slip of paper. Others told of answers received: strength to cope with job or family situations, to adjust to changing circumstances, to face illness with courage.

"It made us more aware of each other's lives and renewed our sense of expectancy about prayer," Rasanen adds. "It gave form and substance to our intercession."

Testimonies in Stereo

When members of First Church of God in Toledo, Ohio, receive an answer to prayer, they're invited to tell the congregation about it. And whenever the incident deals with a family need, both husband and wife come to the microphone to give their individual perspectives.

"Churches get a lot of prayer requests, but not many reports on the results," says Pastor Robert Culp. "That's why we asked a retired woman, Vera Jones, to join our staff as minister of intercession. She keeps track of all the requests, prays for them herself, enlists others to pray — and lines up people to share in the services after an answer has come."

In cases of family difficulty — the illness of a child, or financial pressure, for example — the news of how God sent relief is told from both male and female points of view as couples stand at the front, often with hands joined. "In the black church," Pastor Culp explains, "it seems like women do most of the talking, except for the preacher." (Many white congregations might say the same.) "This is a way we include the men and get them expressing some of their life in Christ."

Vera Jones, because of her close tracking of prayer needs, knows which couples to ask. But other couples come spontaneously now, since the idea of stereo sharing has become common.

Believers' Checkbook

Does prayer actually work? A Peterson, Iowa, prayer group has a better grip on the dynamics of intercession through a unique analogy.

"I was looking for a way to teach the group several key concepts about prayer," says David Hawk, who serves the yoked parish of St. John's United Church of Christ and First Congregational Church. He wanted to emphasize . . .

- That when we pray, it is on Jesus' authority ("in Jesus' name," which brings along the responsibility to discern his will before plunging ahead).
- That prayers need to be concrete and specific.
- That God *does* answer.

His teaching device: a check blank made out to the needy person. The request goes where the dollar amount would normally be written.

Who will meet this request? The check requires a countersignature, so that the bottom line reads, "Jesus Christ BY Prayer Group."

"We pray over these requests," says Hawk, "then insert them in a photo album, where they stay until an answer appears. We review the 'outstanding checks' almost every week when we meet. When a request is accomplished, we write a big red PAID across the front and rejoice at God's faithfulness.

"In a little over a year, we've accumulated a stack of more than 85 PAIDs! A lot of other checks are waiting in the book, but none have been rejected. Our people believe prayer works, because they have solid, visible evidence in this album."

Naturally, the check system is quite a topic of conversation with others and has proven a helpful tool for sharing the gospel with non-Christians, including some state government officials.

MINISTERING TO THE SICK ON SUNDAY MORNING

by Paul A. Cedar, pastor, Lake Avenue Congregational Church, Pasadena, California

I was preaching through the book of James a few months ago when I came to this passage:

"Is any one of you in trouble? He should pray. Is anyone happy? Let him sing songs of praise. Is any one of you sick? He should call the elders of the church to pray over him and anoint him with oil in the name of the Lord" (James 5:13-14, NIV).

How should I handle this text in a large Congregational church? What was it specifically telling us to do?

I thought back to my father, an evangelical Presbyterian pastor, who with my mother believed in praying for their five children when we were sick. I also recalled the words of a marvelous Christian pediatrician who stood next to our first-born son, fighting for his life in an oxygen tent, and gently said, "I've found that the best combination in medicine is the proper blend between penicillin and prayer." We prayed together that day in Denver, and our boy recovered.

Now it was time to continue my expository series in James. I stood in the pulpit and told the congregation about a recent experience in our church family. A deacon's wife had been ill for some time and was not responding to medical treatment. Her husband had asked if some of the pastors and deacons would anoint her with oil and pray for her following a morning service. I was unavailable, but other pastors and some of the deacons had done as he asked. The Lord had responded with wonderful grace and brought healing to her.

So I announced that, from that morning on, our pastoral team and deacons would be available after each of the three services. They would pray for anyone in need of physical, emotional, or spiritual healing, or for broken interpersonal relationships that needed mending. I made my conviction clear that it was not always God's will to heal, but it was always his will for his people to request healing and then to rest in his response.

At the close of the message, I invited any who would like prayer to go to our prayer room after the benediction. A significant number came. Three months later, we were averaging 25 people each Sunday.

Praying goes on quietly and reverently. We do not focus on emotional outbursts or the personality of the church leader who anoints. We focus upon the Lord and seek his will. As D. L. Moody once said, "Spread out your petition before God, and then say, 'Thy will, not mine, be done.' The sweetest lesson I have learned in God's school is to let the Lord choose for me."

We do not plead with God, nor beg or carry on a spectacular event. We simply humble ourselves before the Lord and request his healing in the life of his child. Then we commit that person to our Lord with the conviction that whatever he ordains is right.

As I extend the invitation each week, I tailor it to fit the proclamation of the Word. One Sunday, for example, my message was an exposition of 1 Peter 3:17-22 entitled "Suffering for Doing Good." At the close of the message, I invited people to go to the prayer room if they were hurting and wanted someone to pray with them, if they wished to have prayer for a loved one, if they wanted to know Christ personally as Savior and Lord, or if they wanted to be anointed with oil and prayed for to seek physical, emotional, or interpersonal healing.

Nineteen persons responded. About one third of them requested anointing and prayer for healing.

The healing ministry is also carried on by our pastoral staff and lay leaders during the week as we make hospital visits and call in homes.

The results have been very encouraging. Many people have been healed physically. They have been set free from depression and other emotional ills, while some have received the grace of God in a marvelous measure to continue suffering.

A recent letter from the wife of a young man who has a malignant brain tumor summarizes this ministry. "We want to thank you and our friends at Lake Avenue Congregational Church for praying for us. We feel *bathed* in your love, prayers, encouragement, and help. The peace and grace we are experiencing has been mirrored to the doctors, hospital staff, our neighbors, and my husband's co-workers, many of whom are unbelievers. Pray that our family can learn to live day by day, joyfully trusting and depending on God for each new situation."

This is the most important common denominator of this ministry — the encouragement to entrust ourselves to the Lord and to believe that whether we live or die, we are the Lord's. We trust him utterly.

In Smaller Churches, Too

Some congregations make time for intercession within the worship service itself. Two examples:

The Salvation Army corps on South Campbell in Chicago has reached out to needy persons early in the service. "Soon after the call to worship, while focusing on the Lord and his goodness, I began inviting those with burdens to come forward," says Lt. Bruce Bailey (now reassigned). "The local officers and I would meet them individually, ask for their specific need, and then pray for them quietly."

As in Pasadena, the requests ran a wide gamut: physical, financial, family, relatives, the desire to make a deeper commitment to Christ. "There was never any hesitation," says Bailey. "Some Sundays only one or two would come, but other Sundays as many as 15 responded. Some people walked into the meeting off the street — and came forward for prayer when invited."

While this was going on, the rest of the corps of 50 people sang choruses, meditated with piano background, or joined in prayer as one individual led.

Definite physical healings resulted, Bailey reports. Furthermore, people were encouraged. As one said, "It's refreshing to have someone care about you."

When Freddy Boswell pastored the Union Hills United Methodist Church in Alpharetta, Georgia, he began prayers for the sick as part of Communion.

"We celebrated the Lord's Supper on the first Sunday of the month," he says, "and in Methodist tradition everyone comes to the front to receive the elements. So I began inviting those who desired prayer for healing to come first. Some came for themselves, others on behalf of friends.

"Two or three board members assisted me with the laying on of hands. After everyone received both prayer and the sacrament, they were dismissed, and the rest came to the altar."

Some Sundays, up to a fourth of the congregation responded to the first call, and results were occasionally dramatic. The church's song conductor came requesting prayer for his 10-year-old niece, who had entered the hospital and had been diagnosed to have a brain tumor. She lay in intensive care. Later on, the tumor could not be found, and within a month the girl was out of the hospital.

"Even though this time of prayer takes longer, no one ever complained to me about getting out of church late," says Boswell. "Instead, people thanked me. While standing there with the Communion cup in one hand, my other hand being tightly gripped by people with tears in their eyes, I would say to myself, *This is what church ministry is all about.*

ANYONE FOR FASTING? WELL, YES

by Clyde B. McDowell, associate pastor for pastoral care, Wooddale Church, Richfield, Minnesota

Do ordinary, busy Christians fast anymore?

That was the question that popped into the mind of our board-of-elders chairman, Austin Chapman. Pastor Anderson had mentioned fasting in a sermon, and now the lay leader was getting practical: What about it? Should we — a large, modern church in a Minneapolis suburb — take fasting seriously?

John Wesley once said, "Some have exalted religious fasting beyond all Scripture and reason; and others have utterly disregarded it." We certainly knew which category we were. So we did what any group of uneasy churchmen would do: we referred the matter to the discipleship board for further study.

In a matter of weeks, board member Jeff Jonswold presented a report that didn't let us off the hook at all. He noted, among other things that:

● *Fast* and other forms of the word are used 78 times in Scripture.

● Moses, David, Elijah, Esther, Daniel, Jesus, Anna, the disciples of John the Baptist, Paul, Barnabas, and others all fasted.

● Jesus seemed to think of giving, praying, and fasting as a trio of spiritual disciplines (see Matt. 6:1-18, for example).

Jeff listed four reasons to fast: (1) to better focus the

mind on God; (2) to share, in some small measure, God's own grief over sin; (3) to turn attention away from material needs toward the One who supplies all; (4) to intensify our praying.

He concluded with eight practical guidelines for those who fast (see box).

On September 9, 1980, the paper was officially discussed at a special joint meeting of all boards. Within two weeks, George Penland, chairman of the discipleship board, sent a letter to all who were present encouraging a trial period of prayer and fasting. He asked us to report our experiences and conclusions anonymously.

During the next two months, responses trickled in. One wrote: "I used lunch and supper to dwell upon Isaiah 40 (God's greatness) and Colossians 1 (the same God reached down to us). A very valuable time. It required much discipline and concentration. Nothing magical happened — it's a learning process. Conclusion: I plan to set aside one day a month to fast and pray and meditate."

Another wrote: "It's changed me. I first fasted for a specific prayer request — trying to change God and make something happen. Now, I reflect on God himself. I go to him to have my perspective and attitude changed instead of God's. It has humbled me. My goal is to do it once a week."

One who ate only breakfast for two days wrote: "I was aware of physical discomfort, but I felt that was good. It heightened my awareness and appreciation of God. It's improved my prayer life. I lost weight. I plan to do this again often."

Of those who reported, none were negative or even neutral. All saw fasting as a "helpful," "positive," "uplifting," or "life-changing" discipline.

So the discipleship board voted to take the next step: encourage the church to participate.

On January 28, 1981, Wooddale's first "Day of Prayer and Fasting" was held. People were asked to spend regular mealtimes in prayer for "the nation, its new leadership, our church, the new building project, and our personal lives." We had corporate prayer at the church at 7 A.M., 12 noon, and 7 P.M. I led some Scripture readings and responsive readings in four basic categories: adoration, confession, thanksgiving, and supplication. Hymns and praise choruses were interjected throughout. We prayed in large groups and small groups, sometimes silently, sometimes vocally. Daytime participation was small (20 to 30) but positive. The evening gathering drew 185 (out of a Sunday worship attendance of 1,400). Nevertheless, those who participated were enthusiastic, and many encouraged the idea of all-church fasts.

We held three other fasting days in 1981, with similar numerical responses. We don't know how many joined in private, though there were several.

One homemaker said: "I found it hard at first. But each time I've participated with the rest of the church on the special day, it gets easier and better. Now I'm saying, 'Why didn't I do this before?' "

A business executive says, "I experience no great emotional change on that day, but it does help me focus on a spiritual problem. The change in my daily pattern is a helpful and visible effort to be more involved in prayer. It makes the whole day a time of meditation and spiritual concentration."

One of the pastors says, "It gives me greater spiritual sensitivity. Since I'm disciplining my bodily appetites, I seem to have less temptation — I'm more spiritually in tune." Another pastor adds, "It affects all I do during the day. I learn what it means to 'pray without ceasing.' "

An interesting observation by one church leader gives needed perspective. "There are different reasons for fasting. And if it is part of the regular foundation of our Christian life, we will be ready to fast effectively when crises come and the great decisions of life must be made."

Since then, we have begun to understand this discipline

in our individual and corporate walk with God. We have built a "Day of Fasting" into the calendar for each quarter. We want to rise above mediocrity; we want to experience, through fasting, what Richard Foster calls the "breakthroughs in the spiritual realm that could never be had in any other way . . . (the) means of God's grace and blessing that should not be neglected any longer."

Guidelines for Fasting

1. Reach a personal conviction on the subject through a careful biblical study.

2. Make sure you are medically able to fast before attempting it.

3. Enter with a positive faith that God will reward those who fast with the right motives.

4. Begin with short fasts and gradually move to larger periods of time.

5. Be prepared for some dizziness, headache, or nausea in the early going.

6. Mix your prayer time with Scripture reading and singing or devotional reading.

7. Keep checking your motives during the fast.

8. Break a prolonged fast gradually with meals that are light and easy to digest.

EDUCATION

Peace in the Adult Department

Sometimes adults can be a pain.
- They don't want to be in the same Sunday school class with "those young bucks" or "all those old-timers."
- Once they get comfortable in a class, they don't like being uprooted as *they* get older.
- They especially dislike the subject of birthdays.

So how to divide them up without inciting guerrilla warfare? Phyllis Sloan, director of Christian education at Frisco Church in Webb City, Missouri, recently pulled off a bloodless coup.

"We had classes that were getting older and older, in spite of their designated age category," she says. "Yet we didn't want to go to a total elective system and give up continuity.

"So we surveyed our enrollment and then announced a one-time reorganization, not by age, but by *common interest:* children. The new classes would be permanent from then on, growing through the stages of adulthood together. Nobody would be 'kicked out' when he got to be 40 or whatever. And we'd simply keep adding new classes on the young end."

The current set-up for Frisco's 230 adults is:
- Upper Room Class (those newly married or with preschoolers)
- Families in Training (those who presently have elementary level children)
- Berean Class (those with junior highs)
- New Life Class (those with senior highs and collegians)
- A class of empty nesters
- Three other classes for older adults

The classes chose their own names, being urged to avoid age indications. "Those without children were free to choose the class they found most comfortable," Sloan explains. "In fact, everyone was free to choose; we made it clear we weren't forcing anyone to change. Two or three couples tried the system but elected to go back to a certain teacher or group — and that's all right. Most of the comments, though, have been favorable.

"We still have some work to do," she adds. "For one thing, we need to start a class for middle singles.

"But we're encouraged. The nice thing is you only have to do this rearranging once. Now we're set, with groupings of people who can grow old together."

An Easy Way to Increase Sunday School

Sunday school has been part of the woodwork for so long that many churches forget to invite new people to join it.

When the ushers of Central Baptist Church in Aurora, Colorado, hand you a visitor's card, it includes a separate box to check:

"☐ PLEASE enroll me in your BIBLE STUDY program." The next line asks for date of birth in order to determine class placement.

Does it bring any results? "Since using this card," reports Pastor Danny Williams, "we are enrolling 10 percent of our morning worship visitors — which is 10 percent more than we *were* enrolling! Every time someone checks the box, we send a card that tells what time Sunday school begins, who the person's teacher will be, and what room to go to. And they show up."

In other words, it never hurts to ask.

Baskin-Robbins Bible Study

Prepared Bible study curriculum is nice, but sometimes adult groups like to chart their own course, to study a Bible book without prepackaged questions.

When Louis Haase was at First Presbyterian Church in Toledo, Ohio, and later at Gibson City, Illinois, he found a way to benefit from resources while enjoying free-form discussion.

"Adults want some sort of study aid," he says, "but we thought there could be a better way than the church buying everyone the same book."

His suggestion: get a different commentary for each couple in the class. Haase would go to a Christian bookstore and buy several different laymen's commentaries on the specific Bible book the adult class was going to study. ("We found Barclay and the Laymen's Bible Book Commentary especially helpful," he says.) Then he'd deal them out. Sometimes people in the class also had commentaries at home they'd never gotten around to using, and this gave them the opportunity to discover the treasures already on their shelves.

"The wide variety of viewpoints and writing styles made for lively discussion," says Haase. "We'd have one person summarize the approach of his or her commentary. Then everyone else would compare and contrast. Soon 31 theological flavors had been sampled.

"Of course, the leader has to be a person comfortable with a variety of viewpoints."

When the class was over, books purchased by the church were placed in the church library. That way:

● The library acquired some in-depth Bible study aids.

● Adults were already familiar with the scope of the library's reference works.

Recasting an Old Tradition

In many Sunday schools, opening exercises went out with the hula hoop because, as one wag put it, "they didn't open anything or exercise anybody." Teachers of individual classes made good use of the extra minutes.

But something was lost in the exchange: No one quite had a sense of the whole group anymore. "Our Sunday school has spilled out into two extra houses nearby," says Jan Janofski, director of Christian education at Marquette Gospel Tabernacle in Upper Michigan, "and we never had an occasion to get everyone together."

So the church began a 25-minute special feature for all ages once a quarter, on the fifth Sunday of whatever month had one. Janofski plans each celebration to feature different departments on a different theme. For example:

- "Make a Joyful Noise" — preschoolers played rhythm instruments, others contributed special music.
- "Live What You Learn" — primaries and juniors presented a homemade slide show to illustrate "Tim's Temper," a serialized story.
- "Let Your Light Shine" — adults put on an international breakfast (this even started earlier than usual) to kick off a day-long missions emphasis.
- On another fifth Sunday, junior highs did a skit.

"It's been a tremendous concept with a lot of enthusiasm," says Pastor Louis Ondracek. "The sanctuary has been packed every time because of the advance promotion." Posters, photo mobiles in the foyer, and word-of-mouth previews have all heightened interest.

"People enjoy watching the children perform," says Janofski. "It's almost like a quarterly Sunday school program, only half as long. And we need to be together, so we don't forget who all is meeting at the same hour each week to study God's Word."

A Guest Who Needs No Introduction

Harry Fletcher doesn't teach Sunday school before he preaches. He prefers to spend that time preparing himself in quiet meditation before stepping into the pulpit.

But still he finds his way into each class.

"Whenever we have a guest speaker — six or eight times a year — I teach one of the Sunday school classes," says Fletcher, pastor of York Gospel Center in York, Pennsylvania. "That allows me some personal, direct contact with all age groups."

Fletcher contacts the teacher of the class he'd like to visit several weeks ahead to OK his coming and to ask what the teacher thinks he should talk about.

Recently he discussed God's will with junior highers and spoke to the primary department on "What a Pastor Does."

"When I'm with primaries or younger children, I'm only there for the opening exercises," says Fletcher. "In older groups, I'll have the whole hour."

A few weeks ago, Fletcher spent the hour with the class for the mentally handicapped.

"A baptismal service was coming up, and the teacher wanted me to explain baptism to the students," he says. "So we took them to the baptistry and talked simply about what baptism is and how it's done. The time with that class was one of the highlights of my ministry."

No More Anonymous Teachers

When you take your child to a Sunday school class at Castleview Baptist Church in Indianapolis, you don't have to wonder who's in charge. This church thinks enough of its teaching staff to provide a color picture and a name outside each doorway.

"We wanted to provide recognition for our teachers and also set them up for communication with parents," says David Lohse, minister of education. "So the Sunday school superintendent went around with a 35mm camera and shot pictures, which were then mounted on mat boards. A skilled artist in the congregation added a design border, hand-lettered the teacher's name and department on each one, and sealed the whole thing with clear acetate."

Parents have been quick to praise: "I'm glad you put those up," said one. "Now I know for sure who my child's teacher is."

Even trustees have been heard to say, "That long hallway in the CE wing looks so good — all those smiling faces as you walk along."

On one occasion when a teaching vacancy occurred, Lohse put up the standard rectangle with a blank in the middle, showing only the words "Could this be you?" The post has since been filled.

The posters' personal touch has told both staff and parents that teaching is a significant ministry in this church.

For Adults:
a Piece of the Action

How can the average adult member personally *feel* — and therefore support — what's happening in the church school? How can the gap between sanctuary and children's wing be bridged?

Northwood Presbyterian Church in Spokane, Washington, has seen a dramatic turnaround since a "Church School Chum" program began. Sagging attendance has picked up, adults have become sincerely interested, and warm relationships have been built between kids and grown-ups.

A Church School Chum is basically an adult or teen secret pal who is matched in September with a child, age 3 through 12. Throughout the fall and early winter, the chum writes letters, sends holiday cards, and brings a small wrapped gift for the child each Sunday — a religious bookmark, pencil, cross, poster, paperback, or even an original poem. A box outside each classroom has a list of children on the side, with dates to check off as deliveries are made. At the end of the teaching hour, the secret gifts are passed out.

"Some who volunteer, of course, don't know the children to whom we assign them," says coordinator Flo Cofini, "so we do a bulletin board of children's pictures and names. Anticipation among the children keeps building week by week until mid-December, when we have a grand revealing party." Mysteries are solved; squeals of excitement reign. After that, adult and child continue their friendship by doing things together on Sunday afternoons. The weekly gifts stop, but are replaced by trips to a rodeo or circus, lunches together, and two more special events: a February Valentine party and a March Unbirthday party.

To make the system work, Cofini and her committee also:

- Check the classroom boxes each Sunday.
- Recruit fairy godmothers to provide a cache of extra gifts for visitors and those whose chums forget.
- Telephone chums who forget chronically.
- Publicize the program to the membership.
- Help organize the three chum-child parties.

A large number of adults and teens are thus brought into the weekly Christian education scene. The children know they are cared for. The "family of the church" is fact, not fancy. As the mother of one nine-year-old said, watching him cherish his gift, "David's the luckiest boy in the world."

Pastor John B. Pierce adds, "This has proven to be a successful method for the congregation to live out its baptismal vows to care for the children."

Reported by Lura Goodhue Pierce

What Do Teachers Do?

Guesswork has given way to specifics in the Sunday school of Antioch Baptist Church outside Chapel Hill, North Carolina. Pastor Cris Cannon and the Sunday school director have initiated a one-page teacher's covenant that spells out minimum standards.

The nearly two dozen teachers "seemed actually relieved to have all the expectations on paper," Cannon reports. "Before, people weren't quite sure what was expected, and prospective teachers were always wondering, 'Well, what is involved if I take this job?'"

The covenant asks teachers to commit themselves to do such things as:

- Be able to present the plan of salvation from the New Testament.
- Be in the classroom 10 minutes early and start the class promptly.
- Give adequate time to the actual lesson, not sidelights, announcements, etc. (number of teaching

minutes is designated, depending on age-level).
- Attend one church-sponsored teacher training event during the year and read an assigned text.
- Attend quarterly teachers' meetings.
- Contact absentees monthly.
- Recruit and guide a class outreach leader to enroll new students.
- Incorporate the plan of salvation frequently and the importance of sharing it with others.

The covenant also lists two substitutes upon which the teacher may call; if neither can teach, then the Sunday school director takes over the search.

"At the beginning of the church year in September, we held a special service in which the covenant was explained to the whole church and the teachers made their public commitment," says Cannon. "The church was blessed by realizing what teaching actually means, and the teachers were blessed by the support of the people."

Did any teachers resist signing on the dotted line? "We didn't lose one person from the staff," the pastor says. "A couple of people were not sure about certain items, and this gave the director and me a good opportunity to talk with them.

"For example, one was uneasy about actually asking students to make a decision for Christ. It turned out, in discussion together, that this teacher really hadn't been trained in how to do that. So a need was brought to the surface, and we were able to respond with help.

"The covenant isn't cast in stone; we personalize it in some cases, and we plan to revise it year by year, according to our overall Sunday school goals. It's more than just a legality; it's the teacher entering a responsible relationship with God through his church."

WHY WE MOVED SUNDAY SCHOOL TO SATURDAY

by Harold A. Carter, pastor, New Shiloh Baptist Church, Baltimore, Maryland

Studying the Bible at 9:30 on Sunday morning was a great idea in the days when there was little to do on Saturday night besides take a bath. It may still be a good idea in many parts of the country. But in 1972, as an urban congregation of 2,000 members with fewer than 200 in Sunday school, we had to admit that the traditional format had lost its impact.

The problem was not with the teachers, who were dedicated to their task. Something had happened to the times. Urbanization had eroded community involvement in the local church. Saturday night shopping sprees and family activities were sapping Sunday morning energy. With television filling our society with an entertainment syndrome, it became increasingly clear that an hour of Christian education on Sundays wasn't making the kind of impact needed for our age.

We formed an exploratory committee to come up with specific recommendations to improve the quality of Sunday school. After meeting off and on throughout much of the year, these eight persons urged the church to:

● move the full church school to Saturday between the hours of 10 A.M. and 1 P.M., starting in October, 1973;

● become Bible centered, and supplement basic reference books with literature we wrote ourselves;

● discontinue Sunday school as an organized department and put all energies into Saturday;

- go into the community and publicize widely;
- follow the Christian year in worship;
- consciously seek to be evangelistic and family-oriented.

We decided to take the bold step. Our posters, radio spots, and word-of-mouth advertisement went out. One thousand pupils enrolled the first Saturday, most of them not members of our church.

One of the first unexpected dividends was a swelling tide of evangelism. Parents who sent their children to the Saturday school began coming to the church and were won to the cause of Christ. Whereas New Shiloh had been baptizing around 16 persons a month, we immediately began baptizing an average of 35. We had to move to three full Sunday services — 8:30 and 11:00 A.M. and 6:00 P.M. None of this would have taken place without the Saturday school.

Was it hard to build a staff for the more intensive program? If anything, it was easier. I had worked with Martin Luther King, Jr., as a student at Alabama State Teachers College in the mid-1950s, and I had noticed how trained professionals sacrificed for civil rights causes. Yet many of those persons were apathetic to their local churches. I concluded that trained academic minds needed to be challenged to give their service to Christ.

It was clear that a Saturday church school would call for vastly more dedication and commitment than the traditional Sunday school. It turned out that our professionals — public school and college teachers — rose to the challenge. We faced no vocal objections in organizing the program. In fact, the total church school faculty embraced it with joy. They joined me in wanting to see a renaissance of Christian education in the church.

Neither did we find giving up Saturday to be a problem. After ten years, teachers can still be found talking and fellowshiping with pupils after the 1:00 P.M. closing hour.

A great deal of attention went into planning our schedule. We knew when we started that we would have to keep our teachers inspired and motivated. That meant building in a period for renewal. Therefore we decided to run from September to the end of June each year, and the daily schedule offered variety.

10:00	General Worship
10:30	Bible Study (all classes)
11:30	Second period classes
	Bible
	Recording/writing/arts/crafts/
	typing/cooking/carpentry, etc.
12:30	Assembly — a closing devotion from
	each class

During July, August,and part of September, we cut back to a two-hour schedule, from ten to noon. This has given enough rest to set the stage for an enthusiastic kick-off in the fall each year.

Our church is now alive each Saturday with 400 to 600 students, from Lillious Bryant's infants to senior citizens. In fact, half the attendance is adult, taking classes such a "Learning Things and Going Places" taught by Carrie Shepherd, a retired public school-teacher who introduces community services, available opportunities, and functional skills needed in today's society. For many fathers and mothers, this is their first academic experience in an environment of caring concern. This past fall we made an adjustment in our schedule, releasing the students at 12:30 and spending the last half hour in a teachers' meeting. Here we discuss problems faced in the classes, do training on reaching and keeping new members, and also review the upcoming lesson. If I am in town, I lead this review myself.

One of the greatest spinoffs has been the tutorial program for boys and girls three days a week each July. This uses specialized teachers in the fellowship of New Shiloh. Following this program, students may request Mildred Linear, the coordinator, to assign an ongoing tutor; they then determine the best time to work together. Most of the tutoring happens during the second hour of Saturday church school, always at the church. Tutors are available in math, reading, Spanish, French, typing, Latin, English — and our program is still growing.

Michael Montgomery and Reba Henigan lead a class for the hearing-impaired. A Youth Express class, led by Patricia Morris, is especially designed to meet current problems all teenagers face.

The unifying power behind our Saturday church school is our opening worship service. We seek always to be creative in this period, bringing in from time to time guest choirs, high school bands, preachers, speakers, and persons of note to inspire pupils and help advance the cause of Christ. It has given us a place to train ushers and youth choirs. It has also provided a forum for licentuates in the ministry (we call them sons and daughters of the prophets) to have opportunity to preach the Word.

Highlights of the year include festival days, where teachers set up booths, sometimes blocking off the street in front of the church for an old-time country fair usually built around a family theme. Marches have involved as many as 2,000, celebrating family solidarity in Christ. We have time and freedom to do these kinds of things on Saturday without the artificial barriers that sometimes limit Sunday worship.

All teachers go through a leadership development program before serving. They must be genuinely Christian, evangelical in their beliefs, and committed to the practice of soul-winning and serving others.

A further key is the total involvement of the pastor. I have taught a weekly adult Bible class, sharing truths about various books of Scripture and concerns in Christian theology. This class of 100 has proved to be a nucleus of inner strength and power around which the rest of the program could build.

Several of our men and women, inspired by this class, have gone to seminary to prepare for more effective service.

Seventeen are now pastoring various churches. Another group of women witness weekly in a home for delinquent boys, sharing the Christian faith and serving as big sisters in Christ.

Would we go back to traditional Sunday school? No. We have a catchall class for those who come to our church at 9:30 on Sunday morning, not knowing about our Saturday program. But our dedication is to the ongoing enrichment of the Saturday church school.

We hope to develop home courses for persons unable to attend. A stronger emphasis is now being placed upon moral and ethical development, given the immoral climate of our age. Churches have sent observers from Texas, Virginia, Pennsylvania, Delaware, New York, and the District of Columbia to study our approach to educational renewal. We believe we are on track and want to go forward with renewed zeal.

Tertullian Who?

Do average church members stand in awe of the giants of the faith? Not necessarily. "In one class I referred to Martin Luther," says Mark Littleton, pastor of Berea Baptist Church in Glen Burnie, Maryland, "and a teen-ager wanted to know why I left off his last name — *King*. In my sermons, I started noticing that when I invoked the name of John Wesley, Charles Spurgeon, or George Whitefield in sharp tones, I got only dull looks."

Littleton's solution: a mini-series of 5-10-minute spots every other Sunday night on some important person, event, place, or book Christians should know about.

"Several people have remarked that for the first time they're getting a feel for who's who and what's what in church history," Littleton reports. "The spots also lend much freshness and color to the evening services."

Areas covered:

● Great Christians — writers, preachers, artists, poets, missionaries. Sources: *Walking with the Giants* and *Listening to the Giants* by Warren Wiersbe; *The Norton Anthology of Poetry.*

● Great events with a Christian focus — revivals, the Reformation, church councils, etc. Sources: Works of history by Will and Ariel Durant, Kenneth S. Latourette, Philip Schaff.

● Great hymns and their stories. Sources: E. K. Emurian's *Living Stories of Famous Hymns* and *Forty Stories of Famous Gospel Hymns* (Interlude Books).

The pastor now has members of the congregation doing some of the spot features. "We're getting acquainted with our heritage in drops rather than gallons," he says, "and as a result, it's sinking in. The research is also feeding me with many powerful illustrations I would not have discovered otherwise."

A Class that Spells Relief

How can you help the people in your chuch who live with pain?

The United Methodist Church of Oregon City, Oregon, holds a pain support-study group each Sunday evening. Special speakers, films, and books provide the content for the meetings.

● A pastor who was the victim of three heart attacks has spoken to the group; so has a counselor who works with stroke victims, and a worker from a local crisis center who prays for hurting people.

● One meeting featured the film *Crossbar*, the story of a teenage athlete severely injured and paralyzed in an accident and how he and his family grew closer to God as a result.

● Books sometimes provide encouragement, such as Philip Yancey's *Where Is God When It Hurts?* a penetrating study of why God allows suffering.

Members include people in physical pain, but also those experiencing emotional crises. Divorced people and those disillusioned with life, for instance, are as welcome as the heart attack victim and the rheumatoid arthritic. Usually about fifteen people attend.

A crucial element of the meetings, according to Pastor Wesley D. Taylor, is corporate prayer. One woman, for instance, suffered from an intense muscle ailment she had experienced as the result of chemical injections for Hodgkin's disease. After group prayer, she experienced relief.

"We've had some dramatic stories of healing," says Taylor, "while other people have gradually learned to cope with their continued sufferings."

One pain-ridden arthritic had nearly given up faith in God because of the continued suffering. But through attending the group meetings, this person has been helped to see that God's love is not measured by our comfort, and that we can still believe in him without bitterness.

The group might never have been launched if Taylor himself had not experienced a year and a half of prolonged suffering.

One day, as he was unloading a large radio cabinet at his house, it slipped from his grasp and crushed one of his feet. It cause a severe nerve injury and shut off blood supply to the foot.

For six months, doctors couldn't diagnose the exact problem, and Taylor suffered every day. Finally, nerve specialists pinpointed the injury. By this time Taylor had developed a new sense of empathy for suffering people.

Layers of Bible Study: Reinforced, Concrete

Concerned that random biblical input — one passage of Scripture for Sunday school, another during worship, still another for midweek groups, possibly several more during personal devotions — was creating confusion, Dale Schlafer began to coordinate texts. He discovered, as a fringe benefit, a source of concrete preaching ideas.

The midweek Bible study groups at South Evangelical Presbyterian Fellowship in Denver, called "Women in the Word" and "Men in the Word," began discussing the same text Schlafer would preach the following Sunday.

"We pass out a sheet each Sunday with quiet-time helps for the *following* week's passage," says Schlafer. "These are used as the basis for the midweek discussions."

Schlafer found at least three unexpected benefits:

● More concentration on worship. One layman told Schlafer after a morning service: "When you spoke on John 4 and the woman at the well this morning, I didn't bother to take notes. I already knew the content of the passage. Instead, I was able to focus on worshiping God as the living water."

• More preaching material for the pastor. During the midweek Bible study on John 8, where Christ says, "Before Abraham was born, I am," one man commented on the parallel "I am" statement to Moses in the burning bush.

"Moses had to remove his sandals and hide his face because he was on holy ground," the man observed. "And if Jesus is also 'I am,' then he deserves that same reverence. We're often very flip with Christ, as if he's our buddy. Maybe he deserves our awe, too."

Schlafer used that in the sermon the next Sunday.

• Greater interest in the sermon. "At first I thought having people study the passage before I preached it would steal my thunder," says Schlafer. "But it works just the opposite. We tried it where I'd preach the text before the midweek groups studied it, but as one man put it, 'The senior pastor's already spoken — what's there to discuss?'

"Instead, people look forward to seeing how I handle the text they've already struggled with. If I can use an idea or illustration my group came up with, I'll introduce it with 'Here's one from the group.' People seem to enjoy having a part in the sermon."

Adults Enjoy Back Yards, Too

Children and teens aren't the only ones who like going outside for Bible study. At Lexington Avenue Baptist Church in High Point, North Carolina, the weekly Back Yard Fellowship has become a summer tradition among the adults.

"We wanted to reach the neighborhoods and let people know our church was alive and well during the summer," says Perry Holleman, who was coordinator of church programs at the time. "But with vacations and such, our Thursday night visitation program had dwindled to six or eight people."

Several years ago Holleman dropped visitation during the summer and replaced it with Back Yard Fellowship. It has continued each summer since.

"Each Thursday night now, about 40 people bring their lawn chairs, Bibles, and when possible, unchurched friends to the back yards of volunteering members," says Holleman.

"We would play volleyball, or sing, or share testimonies, or have a devotional time — whatever the host family had planned. Each week we had at least two or three unchurched people come, and one year two families joined our church as a direct result of these fellowships."

The final meeting of the summer is always a surprise. Everyone meets at the church, boards a bus, and takes off for a spot known only to the leader.

"One year we went to Oak Hollow Lake, sat on the bank, and I led the devotional about things that happened along the shores of the Sea of Galilee," says Holleman.

Downtown Devotion

Lunchtime is a good time for spiritual food, too. A church in Kansas has a fresh way of reaching working men, while one in California has found working women eager for midday Bible study.

Several Christian businessmen in downtown Topeka, Kansas, are in the habit of meeting for lunch. When one of them told the group about a series of video tapes he'd seen on "How to Overcome Roots and Strongholds of Sin," the rest wanted to see it, too. But when? Lunch was the only time they were together.

And where? No one lived downtown.

"Why not meet in my showroom during lunch?" asked one, a furniture store owner. "We've got plenty of room around the corner from the main display area, and I've already got TVs and video equipment set up."

So the men, two of them members of Shawnee Heights Baptist Church, ordered the tapes through the church and viewed a tape a week. As word spread, 12-15 men would gather to see the tapes and informally discuss the ideas presented.

When the series ended, they took a couple months off before deciding they wanted to view a series on prayer, which took the next eight weeks.

"It's a low-structure, low-pressure group," says Pastor John Yeats. "We find it works best to have short series, take a break, and come back a few weeks later with another short series."

The men have enjoyed the spiritual input in this unusual setting.

"I gained a new understanding of prayer from the tapes," says one group member. "And I never would have sat down on my own to see them if it weren't for the noon hour group."

For eight years the Fruitvale Community Church in Bakersfield, California, has had a Thursday morning Bible study for women, but the working women felt cut off. So a team from the Thursday study began a Wednesday noon ministry for women who work.

The "Brown Bag Bible Study" met in the basement of a downtown dress shop. The five team members would arrive early to set up tables, tablecloths, and flower arrangements. Pictures were hung on the walls to create a relaxed, homey atmosphere.

Before long, attendance outgrew the dress shop, so now the Brown Bag study meets in the social hall of a racquet club. But the team still brings the flowers, pictures, and tablecloths.

As the women eat their lunches, one of the team members leads a study on a Bible book or topic such as prayer, time management, or helping people in crisis. Everything is done within 35 minutes so the women can be back at work promptly.

"Wednesday noon is an oasis in my week," says one working woman. "It's a great place to get away from the pressure of work for a few minutes."

Periodically, the group holds a salad luncheon, with nothing on the agenda but informal conversation. "Those are the times lots of newcomers attend," says one of the team members.

Approximately a third of the group is unchurched, and over 35 churches are represented by women regularly attending.

"We emphasize the unity we have in Christ," she says. "We try to glorify him. By organizing this ministry, those of us who aren't working can meet the needs of the women who are."
Reported by Robert L. Brady, Jr.

An Upbeat Start for Couples' Class

A good interaction question to open a Sunday school session on the family: "Tell one thing your spouse is doing right in raising your children."

When they used it at Village Green Baptist Church in Glen Ellyn, Illinois, "it turned the whole session into a positive experience," says Ron Salzman. "You could just see spouses respond to being complimented by their mate in front of a group. And furthermore, a lot of good insights were shared."

SERVING

"What Would You LIKE to Do?"

A few years ago, Pastor Paul Neal dared to ask his people at Summitview Church of the Nazarene in Kansas City for their honest preference about service in the church.

After a sermon on life stewardship, he passed out a Christian Service survey card to everyone present, on which they marked their various talents. But then he said, "If you could do the one thing in the church that you prefer to do more than anything else, what would it be? Put an asterisk beside that one thing." The people were invited to come forward and place their cards on the altar as symbols of a "living sacrifice" (Rom. 12:1).

"We placed more people in ministries they really *wanted* to be in as a result of that," says Dr. Kenneth S. Rice, a denominational executive who was on leave with the church's staff and had given Neal the idea. "Imagine our surprise when we saw the trustee chairman's card: He wanted to work with boys' and girls' clubs! He had been an Eagle Scout as a teenager. But because he was now an outstanding businessman, he always seemed to get elected to high office at the annual meeting.

"We gave him the opportunity to work with kids aged 6 to 12 on Wednesday nights. The club program thrived, the attendance doubled, and he was more fulfilled than he had dreamed possible."

Who said ministry had to be all work and no fun?

Church Is a
Many-Splendored Thing

*Sometimes a church's best parts go unnoticed by the people
who would most benefit from them. Here's what two
congregations did to highlight their various ministries:*

St. Simons United Methodist Church off the coast
of Georgia threw a "Ministry Fair" one Sunday morning,
with 14 different booths. "Our Council on Ministries
had decided to try to better inform the congregation on
what we were doing to fulfill our purpose," says Richard Whitaker, program director. "One way we got
people's attention was through a highly publicized
fair."

As members wandered from site to site they
- saw slides of the senior high summer work camp
in western North Carolina,
- learned about making a will at the stewardship
exhibit,
- viewed photos and children's artwork from the
weekday school,
- thumbed through the materials to be used in a
Bethel Bible Series just beginning,
- picked up brochures on the church's mission involvement and giving,
- found out what the new young-adult fellowship
was planning for Sunday school and evening activities,
- had their blood pressure taken at the
health/welfare display, and decided whether to sign up as
a blood donor.

The fair, which was open from 9 A.M. to 1 P.M., included junior highs dressed as clowns and storybook
characters who entertained the children, greeted
worshipers at each service, led dances and songs, and put
on a puppet show. One Sunday school class took on
the job of providing refreshments. Senior highs ran

outdoor football throws and basketball tosses for children while their parents browsed.

"Attendance held fairly constant throughout the four hours except for a bulge during Sunday school," Whitaker reports. "From the comments, smiles, and armfuls of handouts being carried away, we could tell the fair was a success. We hope to do it again in a few years."

A week earlier in downtown Minneapolis, worshipers entering the Central Free Church on Sunday evening received a brochure and coupon booklet called "Service Opportunities 1982-1983." A typical coupon read:

> *I would like to be involved in the FRIENDSHIP TEAMS ministry. I realize that I may submit this coupon anytime during the year and have decided to do so now. I look forward to hearing more information about this ministry.*
> *Sincerely,* _____

Tim Johnson, minister of congregational development, led the service that evening, giving a 15-minute meditation on the concept of lay ministry. Then came a slide show that featured eight programs: a hospitality outreach, greeters, sponsors for newcomers, conversational meals, Central Ambassadors (music/drama teams), ministry to collegians, Partners in Prayer, and Friendship Teams to visit the elderly.

"These were all extra chances to serve, in addition to our constitutional set-up of committees and Christian education posts," Johnson explains. "Following the slides, I explained how to fill out the coupons — and then we passed the offering plate. We weren't collecting money; we were collecting people's time and energy."

Johnson wound up with approximately 80 coupons out of an audience of 150. He promptly sorted the names and scheduled briefing sessions with most of the groupings for 15-20 minutes following a morning service in order to spell out details and introduce lay coordinators.

"We've done this for three years," says Johnson. "Our people are steadily growing in their willingness to put their names on the dotted line and commit themselves to some form of ministry as Christians."

STAYING CLOSE WITH ALL THE MEMBERS

by Evelyn Collum, Pomona, California

"How can we, as a church, serve you and your family today?"

It is a question so simple, so artless, that it is almost naive in the busy 1980s. Would it not surely bring down an avalanche of requests?

But it is precisely the question that is breaking the ice in large congregations — churches a cynic might say are too successful to reach out to individuals anymore. Can small-town concern and neighborly love survive in the smog of greater Los Angeles? A ministry called Telecare responds, "Yes."

Telecare is nothing more than a group of trained lay people dedicating themselves to phone each member on the roll, from A straight through to Z, and offer aid, encouragement, and support. In so doing, they convey the powerful message that individuals are more than names on a computer printout or numbers on packets of offering envelopes.

The responses range from surprise to shock.

"God must have known I needed to hear from you just now."

"Did someone tell you to call me? How did you know I'm going through one of the worst times of my life?"

And later: "It worked! You prayed for me over the phone, and God answered."

We started Telecare at 3,750-member First Baptist Church in Pomona two years ago. Since then the concept has spread to two other congregations nearby. Each is attempting to call each member four times a year, except for widows, widowers, the seriously ill, and the bereaved, whom we call more often.

Teleministers come to the church office to make their calls, working three- to four-hour shifts in the morning, afternoon, or evening, so as to reach the entire membership. Whenever they discover a practical need, they do what they can to match that need with the gifts of others in the body.

For example, a woman I'll call Sharon was slipping deeper and deeper into depression. Her 21-year-old son had a malignant brain tumor, and each time we called Sharon we kept suggesting ways for her to get help. But even visits to her home did not penetrate her isolation.

Finally she got so down she lost her job. The last time we called, she was lying on her bed alone, crying.

About that time, a member of the church called Telecare offering transportation if anyone needed a ride to the services. As an afterthought, she asked if we could use a professional clown.

While she was explaining what she did, Sharon came to mind. The next day, the clown visited Sharon with a big bouquet of helium balloons, a contagious smile, and the message that God loved her and so did her church.

That very afternoon, *Sharon called us* to ask about counseling. At last she was reaching out for help, and her healing began.

On another day, we called a single mother of two young boys. When we asked how the church could help her, she had a ready request: Could we do anything about the exposed electrical wiring in her apartment? She had tried to get the manager to make repairs but had failed.

We assured her we cared about her family's well-being, and we would ask God to lead someone to put love into action and help her. We then went to our files and began calling people who had offered to share the gift of helps. Within two calls, we found a member who would make the repairs.

Soon the mother was on the phone thanking us and God for an answer to her prayers. She offered to teach sewing and guitar to anyone, without charge. Telecare now had another resource.

These kinds of experiences laid to rest our initial fears about whether our calls would be welcomed or not. Not one time in thousands of calls has anyone treated us as an intrusion or brushed us off for being nosy.

At first, people weren't sure whether to believe we were really willing to serve them. They trusted us to pray with them, which we often did, but they hesitated to ask anything of us.

We eased their doubts by explaining we could only promise to give God the opportunity to be our matchmaker, finding resource people to meet needs. We promised that our Prayermates, a group of lay ministers with the gift of intercession, would pray daily about the needs we discovered.

The two congregations that began Telecare after we did learned from us. Both pastors prepared their people with pulpit explanations and publicity. Members knew what to expect, and the calls were received from the beginning with warm anticipation.

Says David Burns at Hillside Community Church in Alta Loma, "As a pastor, I am encouraged because I know the members are caring and praying for one another. Both the Teleministers and the members deepen their spiritual lives. They see firsthand the role of prayer — it really works. For some, this is their first encounter with answered prayer."

Each Telecare program has a director, somewhat like a director of volunteers. Our training program takes five sessions of 2½ hours each:

● The Teleminister's devotional and prayer life, with emphasis on spiritual maturity, intercession, and what it means to depend on the Holy Spirit.

● Active listening; role playing and feedback. We use

material from Crystal Cathedral's New Hope crisis telephone line ministry.

- Building trust over the phone; specific ways to lessen fear and break down protective walls, especially in the first seconds of the call.

- Components of the call: openings and closings, the use of Scripture, handling prayer requests, filling out forms. During this lesson people listen to the trainer make actual calls and then discuss what happened.

- Review of previous sessions, plus trainees making calls themselves, with close supervision.

In order for a caller to get past the "I'm fine" facade, we teach loving responses such as "I'm glad you're doing so well. It's been three months since we've talked, and a lot can change in that period of time. In my own life [caller gives an example of change], and I found I really needed support during that time. That's one reason I'm calling you today to see if I can pass along the support and care that was shared with me during my difficulty. . . ."

More often than not, this self-disclosure breaks down the protective shield. People want to be loved and understood.

Telecare has touched the lives of hundreds of our members. The junior highs got involved doing yard cleanup for the elderly. Other Sunday school classes painted a widow's home, roofed a garage, and built a wheelchair ramp for a stroke victim.

We set up a bank of jobs needed and jobs available. We did the same thing for apartments and houses.

Some of those who volunteered to help in torn-up family situations have been able to bring healing. There have been first-time commitments to accept Christ as Lord. Communion has been taken to heretofore unknown shut-ins. Others were provided with rides to the doctor, to church, and to shopping. Both givers and receivers have been abundantly blessed in the process.

In fact, Hacienda Heights Baptist Church now has a

waiting list of members who want to be Teleministers. The calls have touched their own lives so personally that they want to join the ministry. Meanwhile Pastor Bill Tipton sets aside a block of time each month to go over the call reports and reflect on the needs of his congregation.

The prime value of Telecare is that it uncovers needs people are too upset or too timid to mention on their own. In the middle of a call to a man one day, he suddenly asked if Telecare would call his married daughter. We gently probed for more information, but all he would say was "She could use a call."

We dialed her number. It was busy — all afternoon.

Finally, we got through and asked if there was something the church might do to help her.

The young woman burst into tears. Right at that moment, she said, she had just decided to give up on her marriage, her kids, and God. We shared God's love for her as well as our love and concern. We assured her she was not alone in her pain. We were there to pray with her and help in any other way we could.

Today, she credits that phone call with saving her marriage and her faith.

"Telecare is the stethoscope which hears the pulse of the congregation in order to bring help, hope, and love to its members," a recent newsletter at Hillside explains. "It is the way Hillside Community Church has chosen to say, 'We sincerely care for you, and we want to serve you in whatever way God provides.'"

Deacons on Call

Helping people in financial straits is often time-consuming — and pastors are busy people. That's one reason why the Christian Reformed Church in Elmhurst, Illinois, has put it benevolence caring almost entirely in the hands of deacons.

"We reorganized our consistory a couple of years ago," says Rob Petroelje, deacon chairman, "to align with our various spiritual gifts. We ended up with three groups: shepherd/elders, ministering deacons, and an administrative group of both elders and deacons."

The nine ministering deacons apply the gift of showing mercy to two areas:

● Within the church — meals to the sick, clothing, child care, and cash as needed. Deaconesses help in this area as well. The church has an unusual program of regular subsidy to some of its elderly in rest homes, currently totaling $1,000 every month.

● Outside the church. When calls come about families or individuals in a crisis, the church office notifies Petroelje, who assigns one or two deacons to determine the needs. "We go and talk to the people. Do they need food? We take them to the grocery store right then. Do they need to be put in touch with a public agency? We guide them through the process. Naturally, since these are strangers to us, we have to be discreet, but we'd rather err on the side of generosity than stinginess. After all, Jesus' parable of the sheep and goats in Matthew 25 is essentially about reaching out to strangers."

On a recent Thursday, Petroelje was called to help a young couple being evicted that very night. "We put them up overnight in a YMCA, then found temporary housing for a week. By then we'd located an apartment for them, and we financed them through the two weeks it took to get onto Public Aid. The woman was pregnant, so some of our women met with her to give prenatal counseling. Meanwhile, an auto repair shop owner in our church was able to give the husband a part-time job.

"After about three or four weeks, we asked if they'd be willing to have members of our evangelism team call on them. They said yes. She had been an irregular attender of another church, while he didn't go at all. From that night on, they've been in our church almost every Sunday."

Sometimes the reverse happens: people come to the church seeking spiritual help — visitors to the women's coffee fellowship, for example — and then financial needs come to light. "The physical and spiritual outreaches go hand in hand," says Petroelje.

The church's benevolence outreach is funded by a second offering every other Sunday morning. Besides the assistance for the elderly, the fund sees another $300-350 come in and go out monthly. Pastor Wayne Leys meets with the deacon chairman each month for consultation and updating, but the bulk of the face-to-face helping is done by lay people.

Sharing the Abundance

When springtime comes, some Sunday morning churchgoers exchange not only handshakes but cauliflower and crocuses. Bidwell Memorial Presbyterian in Chico, California, and Wesley United Methodist in Charleston, Illinois, are but two congregations that set out a produce table each week from May through October.

"Most of the churches in Chico do this," says Diane Caldwell, church secretary, "since the Sacramento Valley is such an abundant growing area. One of our older women named Elizabeth Rummell takes charge of our table, receiving people's donations of extra food and flowers and helping others select what they can use."

The California church sets up on the front lawn

near where coffee is served, while the Illinois church puts its table just inside the building. None of the items are priced, but both congregations provide a container for donations, which are applied to hunger relief.

"Some of us have large gardens," says Rose Mary Shepherd, who chairs the administrative board at Wesley Church, "and this is our way of sharing with those who don't. We started this in the summer of 1980, and there's always an abundance, from the early lettuce to the pumpkins and gourds in the fall."

Shepherd makes two suggestions for those starting such an exchange:

1. Prime the pump at the beginning by personally asking people with gardens to bring their surpluses. "It takes a while to get rolling," she says, "but once the habit is established, people will do it automatically."

2. Have bags available for those taking food home.

Both women say leftovers are seldom a problem; the tables are clean by the end of the morning. "It's been a help to apartment dwellers and others who don't have a chance to grow their own food," says Diane Caldwell. "And what money it generates goes to the poor."

Lending More than an Ear

Whom do you ask if you need to borrow an electric sander? A fondue pot? Or if you need help tuning your car, or housing guests from out of town?

Who won't think you're imposing?

At Good Shepherd Community Church in Woodridge, Illinois, members have to look only as far as the lists of possessions and services people are willing to share.

"About a year ago, after a series of sermons and a retreat focusing spiritual gifts, a man in a congregation said,'We not only have spiritual gifts to share with each other, but physical gifts, too.' We agreed, and these lists developed to facilitate that sharing," says Pastor David Armstrong.

One list itemizes possessions for loaning: tools, kitchen appliances, even an old station wagon.

A second list names people willing to perform specific services: car repair, painting, typing, baby sitting, haircuts, sewing, lodging overnight guests, watching pets and plants for vacationers, plumbing, photography, and housework.

"Last summer our family went camping for the first time," says Armstrong. "We contacted the Chadwicks, who were listed under camping equipment, and they set us up with sleeping bags and air mattresses. Another member provided a tent."

In turn, the Armstrongs were called recently by a young woman who needed someone to look in on her dog and two parakeets while she was on vacation.

Now, about that fellow with the pet tarantula . . .

The People Bank

Church work, like housework, is never done. There's always something more that needs doing.

That fact scares volunteers, who are afraid of offering themselves to the church and finding the time demands more than they can afford.

A "People Bank" solved the problem at Sligo Seventh-day Adventist Church in Takoma Park, Maryland. Rhonda Visser, community services director, realized many church ministries needed help for just a few hours a month.

"We told the congregation that Rhonda needed commitments for one to three hours a month from 25 people," says Pastor James Londis. "To our surprise, 45 people signed up. Apparently, when members know in advance exactly how much time they are committing, they are willing."

The short-order ministries include
- picking up used furniture and delivering it to needy families,
- tending an elderly invalid so her son can have a morning off,
- sorting and putting away canned goods collected by the church children for the needy,
- providing transportation for elderly folks to doctor's appointments.

"We now have over 60 people we can contact for short-term ministries," says Visser. "I promise to call them only once a month, and I send out thank-you notes periodically to those in the People Bank. Those two things have helped make it successful."

Quick with a Quiche

Carry-in meals for new mothers get arranged with a minimum of fuss at College Church in Wheaton, Illinois, thanks to an efficient tradition in the young-couples Sunday school class.

The understanding is: parents of each newborn receive five meals to allocate as they wish.

"After a baby arrives," explains Mary Gieser, wife of the class president, "I simply call the mom and ask which nights she'd like us to cover. Depending on when her mother or mother-in-law arrives or goes home, she can space out the meals to her best advantage. Some request all five in a row, Monday through Friday, while others use them over a couple of weeks."

The next Sunday morning, the Giesers pass around a sign-up sheet showing name, address, and the five designated evenings. Five volunteers are thus easily re-cruited, and all the information is there in their lap.

"Even if a baby is born early in a week — say, on

Monday," Gieser explains, "the mother and child aren't likely to go home from the hospital until nearly the weekend, when the dad can help. And by Sunday, our system is up and running."

The Moving Crew

When moving day arrives, people have always helped their neighbors pack and unpack. But at the Riverdale Presbyterian Church in suburban Atlanta, the kindness is not left to chance. A work crew of four to five members is enlisted by a central coordinator.

"It started about eight years ago, when two very active families in the church were moving away at the same time," Pastor Cecil Murphey remembers. "People were genuinely sorry to see them go and wanted to do something to show their love. So we got together and helped them load their trucks."

Since then, a list of men on call has grown to 25, and they've averaged a move a month up until the recent recession, which discouraged relocation. "We're in an area with a number of apartment complexes," says Murphey, "and many young couples come in and rent for a year or two, then try to buy a home. So we help them move."

Besides the muscle, another church family provides a one-dish meal — chili or a casserole — to feed the weary movers at the end of the day. A real sense of camaraderie has developed among the crews over the years.

"We make no charge," Murphey adds. "If people want to give something, we suggest they donate to the church's hunger fund.

"Once in a while, we move a needy family that's outside the congregation, after a referral from a community agency. This is a practical way to help others as well as our own."

Where Needs Get Action

The problem: how to connect givers of practical household items with those in need — without offending either one and without creating a lot of red tape.

For several years now, furniture, clothing, and all kinds of accessories have been flowing back and forth at Homewood Full Gospel Church in Illinois through a simple "Blessing Board" in the narthex. Two sets of cards are available for anyone to fill out and post on the two sides of the board: "Blessings" and "Needed Blessings." Whenever someone in the congregation of 700 notices a "Needed Blessing" he could fill, he takes the card and makes contact; whenever someone sees an object or item he could use, he does the same.

"The board seems to take care of itself — nothing has to run through the church office," says Walter Pedersen, pastor. "Yet it helps us all know what the needs are in our fellowship and do something about them."

What distinguishes this board from those at the local supermarket or Laundromat is that nothing is for sale here. No rentals are announced or services hawked. "We just want to share our abundance with one another," says Skip Vogel, church secretary. She remembers the very first exchange: a piano from a church family to a Spanish church being launched. "Not long ago," she adds, "a faithful young couple in the church was facing the arrival of their first baby — with no insurance because of unemployment. A note on the Blessing Board resulted in a *total* outfitting — baby clothes, a crib, a high chair, a wind-up swing, even maternity clothes for the mother! They were just overwhelmed.

"Now that the baby has arrived, this couple is already giving some of the things they received to others in need through the Blessing Board. That's what we love to see happen."

Round Trip Guaranteed

Bentley Creek Wesleyan Church in upstate Pennsylvania endeared itself to its pastoral family a few summers ago with an unusual gift at vacation time. Pastor and Mrs. Bradley Wood had decided to take one last extended camping trip before their son and daughter, 15 and 12, got involved in summer jobs and then college life.

The Sunday morning before they left for the West Coast, the church treasurer suddenly came striding toward the pulpit at the end of the announcements. In one hand was a shiny five-gallon gasoline can. As the speechless pastor stepped aside, the man announced, "We want you to have a good vacation. But we also want to make sure you have enough gas to get back to us. So here's a little help."

Wood gratefully received the can, even though it seemed empty. Only when he unscrewed the cap did he discover the contents: 184 dollar bills.

"We had a great vacation," Wood remembers, "with warm thoughts about the congregation back home. And we still have that gas can around to remind us of their love."

Reported by Patricia Wood

Humbling Yourself in the Sight of the Town

On one side stands the church — pure, righteous, aloof. On the other side, the community — motley, problem-plagued, but wary. How to bridge the gap?

Here are accounts of two churches, the first in South Dakota, the second in Washington, who reached out by

becoming servants to their towns. Their work was lowly —
but noticed.

Since the spring of 1982, Sunshine Bible Church
and Academy has spent a day cleaning up the ditches of
the four highways leading into the county seat of
Miller. Not just the teenagers with strong backs —
everyone.

"We wanted to do more than just wait for people to
come to us," says Pastor Doug Roberts. "We wanted to
show them what an active, unified church looks like."

More than 100 people got involved, a third of them
adults. Roberts divided them into teams, dropping them
off at preplanned points in the country and having
them work their way toward the city limits. "You can
cover about five miles of ditch in two hours," he says.
Last year the group cleaned up 32 miles altogether.

The bottles, cans, and paper were bagged separately
so that some could be sold to the local recycling center,
netting more than $75. After the work was done, eve-
ryone gathered for a picnic.

"All ages can work in this kind of serving," says
Roberts. "If older folk don't want to do all that bending,
they can drive the pick-ups up and down the road
gathering bags. Or they can prepare food and get the fire
started at the picnic site."

The event has drawn media attention throughout
South Dakota as well as accolades from high places —
bankers, the mayor, and even the governor of the
state. "As a result, some from the community have said
they'll come help us next time."

When Chad McComas led a similar event at the
Vancouver (Wash.) Seventh-day Adventist Church, it involved only youth — but it was used as a fund raiser.

"We needed new chairs in our department, and we
didn't want to sell candy," he says. "Other groups were
doing walk-a-thons, but we thought, 'What useful
purpose do they accomplish? Can't we raise money and
benefit somebody at the same time?' "

That's when they settled on a litter-a-thon. They asked the highway department for a stretch of road that needed cleaning and, understandably, got an enthusiastic response. The officials even donated trash bags and sent trucks to pick them up once they were filled.

Meanwhile, the teens asked relatives and friends to pledge up to a dime per pound of garbage collected.

"My wife and I were kept busy driving up and down the road weighing bags as kids filled them up," says McComas. "Many collected more than 100 pounds of garbage, and by the end of the day we'd raised over $500. We were also able to keep the aluminum cans for recycling."

In this case as well, the governor sent congratulations; each student received a certificate of appreciation.

Working Wonders

When jobs are scarce and several families in your church need employment, what can you do?

New Testament Baptist Church in Centralia, Illinois, took inventory of the skills within the congregation and decided to try to drum up work for its jobless. The church put a small classified ad in the local newspaper.

FREE ESTIMATES: Roofing, painting, carpentry, decorating, plumbing, murals, sign painting, and auto repair. For better quality at better prices call 532-0435.

"We prayed for God to bless the ad," says Pastor Charles Frick. "Calls began coming into the church office, and after six weeks, all the men were employed on different contract jobs."

In addition, Frick reports an unexpected blessing to the church. Attendance and offerings were up 25 percent as the excited reemployed brought friends and relatives to services.

"One Sunday we had three saved and two come for

baptism," he says. "There's a wholesome enthusiasm among the people as we watch the Lord performing a miracle. Especially the young families have grown closer together and are supportive of one another."

The Job Finders

Church newspaper ads usually tout upcoming services. But the Fridley Assembly of God ad in the April 6, 1983, *Minneapolis Star and Tribune* mentioned only the services of its unemployed. And it wasn't on the religion page. It ran in the business section.

Personnel Department:
We'd like to help you find the right person for the right job. When you advertise you are inundated with applications. This consumes a lot of your very valuable time.

You may find the person you need by looking over the summary of résumés we have on file. There is no fee to you or the people using this service. We, as a church, are simply trying to match the needs of employers with the needs of people.

Then the phone number of the suburban Twin Cities church was listed.

This novel approach to helping jobless members began in March when church member Melvin Wolf, himself out of work, led seminars on résumé writing, how to look for work, and how to interview. The idea of using the church as a no-fee clearinghouse was his brainchild. Pastor Mark Denyes was an enthusiastic supporter.

One Sunday Denyes announced the church was setting up a file of résumés to send to area businesses, and all unemployed people should meet in the church office next Wednesday night and bring their résumés.

"There was a tremendous round of applause," says Denyes. "People felt finally we were doing something about unemployment."

On Wednesday, 20 people jammed Denyes's office to discuss strategy. Church secretaries helped those who couldn't type. Then the résumés were sorted and catalogued.

Besides placing the $469 newspaper advertisement, the church mailed the announcement to 60 local companies, providing a synopsis of the skills available.

Other church members took the synopsis to their employers and also alerted the church office to job openings at their companies. As word spread, jobless neighbors of church members also added their résumés to the file.

A dozen firms have contacted the church to request résumés, and "all but three or four of the unemployed have now found jobs, some through other sources," says church secretary Betty Anderson.

Reported by Fred Sindorf

NO WINGS, BUT A LOT OF PRAYER

by Kenneth C. Carter, Jr., pastor, First United Methodist Church, Carrollton, Texas, with Joel B. Green

We'd heard rumors that Braniff International was in trouble, but when the Dallas-based airline suddenly folded its wings in May, 1982, it still shocked us.

Some 9,000 people found themselves without jobs, and that wasn't counting those laid off earlier as Braniff began curtailing services. In our church in suburban Dallas, more than 20 families were affected. Some members were pilots, others were upper-level management, and still others were reservation and support personnel. In some cases both husband and wife suddenly joined the ranks of the unemployed.

The economic crisis experienced by these families is obvious. Not so obvious, but also a major problem, are the emotional upheavals caused by loss of security, feelings of inadequacy, and the shock of career change.

We discovered, however, that the situation gave our church the opportunity to be truly the body of Jesus Christ. Since the church is in the business of helping needy people, here was a chance to expand our ministry. Our people responded quickly.

Bob Sewell, our lay associate for evangelism, immediately compiled a list of our affected members. Within two days of the shutdown, each family was contacted by phone or in person to determine their needs.

In some cases, employees had been expecting layoffs and

had other jobs already lined up. Others, however, were desperate to find work.

With the information in hand, the church developed a strategy. The plan, administered primarily by Smith Noland, lay associate for counseling, worked on several fronts.

- *An informal employment bureau.* Those without work were encouraged to update their résumés and place copies in the file in the church office. We also spread the word to prospective employers within the church. The file was then used to match those hunting jobs with those looking for employees.

This informal approach was all it took for some people.

Jeanie Morgan, for instance, a 13-year Braniff employee in reservations, had no idea what she would do when the airline folded. But within a week, she was hired by another member of the church to manage a franchise in his chain of popcorn stores.

- *Counseling services.* Early rumors of Braniff's financial squeeze had warned many of the employees.

"There was, in fact, a sense of relief at the announcement," said Noland. "No longer did they have to wonder, 'What will happen?'"

But that relief didn't prevent many from feeling tension, anxiety, even anger when the full impact of their loss of employment hit them.

All of us on the pastoral staff took the initiative to approach the former Braniff employees to say, "I know this must be a tough time for you. If you'd like to come in and talk about it and pray together, I'm available."

We sought them out before the crisis forced them to come to us. Many took us up on the offer.

- *Financial assistance.* Depending on the needs of individual families, financial support was given. In some cases, where new jobs have been slow to materialize, financial help continues.

In one family, both the husband and the wife lost their

jobs with Braniff. She was expecting a child, and when the baby was born, medical complications arose. Our members, through the church's emergency fund, provided help with car payments, doctor's bills, and rent.

Fortunately the husband landed a job as a management trainee in a fast-food chain owned by a Christian businessman in the area.

In other cases, Sunday school classes gave money directly to their members who were hurt by the layoffs.

How were these measures received?

Randall States, a former Braniff pilot, said that he and his family have benefited most from the encouragement and personal support of individual church members.

After Braniff shut down, States was offered a job with the computer firm where his wife worked. While wrestling with the decision whether or not to enter this totally new career, members of his Sunday school class called and wrote notes to encourage him and assure him of their prayers.

"We felt loved," States said. "It was great to see the family of God at work."

The crisis had an impact on the whole church fellowship. Our people saw that in tough circumstances they have an opportunity to live out their faith — to *do* something with their Christianity.

An economic crisis gave us a real-life situation to practice what we'd been studying in Ecclesiastes 4:10 about lifting up the brother who is down.

Our fellowship has become a resource, a caring, active support community. Because our people expressed their faith in love, our congregation was enabled to be the body of Christ.

Unemployment was the means God employed to get our church to put love to work.

Youth and Adults in Action

Usually service expeditions are confined to groups of youth or else adults. But St. John's United Methodist Church, Paradise, Pennsylvania, combines all ages past junior high in its semiannual work trip to the Appalachian Mountains.

Every two years a group of eight to eighteen from the church help a United Methodist parachurch organization build houses for needy folk in the mountains.

"The age mix is a real plus," says Mary Carrigan, a group leader since 1972. "We have the freshness of youth and the experience of age on our trips." Ages range from 16 to 70 years old.

They leave Paradise on a Saturday morning, stop overnight at a Methodist church along the way, and arrive at their destination by Sunday noon.

They live in a one-room bunkhouse, joining other church groups who have come for the same reason.

The parachurch group instructs them about what jobs they are to perform and where. The routine chores include putting up drywall, paneling, painting, puttying windows, and even building outhouses.

One year the Paradise group helped a man who was an alcoholic; he lived in an old chicken house with cardboard walls. The group completely rebuilt his home, and in the evenings when he would come home from work, they spent time with him, sharing and living their Christian testimonies.

"This man was so touched that a bunch of people would help him," says Carrigan, "that from the time we got there until the time we left, he did not touch one drop of alcohol."

According to Carrigan, some of the more visible benefits of the trip occur in the group members themselves. "Those who go are completely changed by the conditions they witness firsthand," she points out. "Some have gone into social work as a result of their involvement."

Carrigan and her husband, who is pastor of the church, use the opportunity to counsel, encourage, and get better acquainted with their parishioners who join the group. "We travel together, have devotions together, and grow closer together," she adds.

Each group member raises money for the trip. Car washes, odd jobs, and donations from people in the church raise nearly $2,500.

"If there's money left over after our expenses are paid," Carrigan says, "we give it to the organization that heads up the program."

PRISONERS ON THE LOOSE

by William J. Furr, pastor, Trinity Baptist Church, Raleigh, North Carolina, with Anita Moreland Smith

What our middle-class congregation knew about prisoners wasn't much. Five or six of our people had served as counselors during a Bill Glass in-prison crusade once. Other than that, we didn't know what to expect when Tom Metts, Prison Fellowship's southeast regional director, suggested we host six inmates for a two-week community service project.

"Are they dangerous?" the board of deacons wanted to know, understandably. The answer was no, for two reasons: (1) these men had become active Christians, and (2) they'd been incarcerated for nonviolent crimes in the first place — counterfeiting, embezzling, selling stolen property.

Most of their days would be spent winterizing the homes of poor people as a form of restitution. What were we to do for the prisoners? Welcome them. Sponsor a dinner for them their first night in town. Put them up in our homes, invite them to participate in our services. Be their friends. Hold a final dedication service at the end of the two weeks, with Chuck Colson as the speaker.

We took a deep breath and told Tom, "OK — count us in."

On Sunday, October 17, 1982, they arrived from Maxwell federal prison in Alabama and Eglin in Florida. By the end of that first meal, we knew there was no reason to fear David McIntyre, Donny Sauls, Bob Fowler, Jerry Morgan, Bob Matters, and Wilson Johnson. These were solid

Christian men who only wanted to use their beliefs and talents to help others.

They shared the five reasons why they had come:

- To be discipled and to grow in their faith through serving.
- To show communities like ours an alternative to locking people up.
- To challenge us to get involved in ministering to the poor.
- As federal prisoners on a release program, to demonstrate how the same thing could be done on the state level.
- To help Prison Fellowship staffers and volunteers raise our awareness of involvement in prison ministry.

Tom Metts said, "These men want to prove they are caring people. Not all prisoners are the TV image — callous, cold, hardened. The average inmate is concerned about what he's done and wants to right the wrong."

The next morning, after an hour of Bible study, the crew went to work. Seven inner-city homes had been selected on the basis of low income combined with high utility consumption in the past. Carolina Power and Light donated all the supplies — insulation, storm windows, caulking, lumber.

Mary Green, 82, wasn't sure at first that she wanted convicted felons in her attic, but she soon changed her mind.

"I've been living here since 1957 and never had it insulated," she said. "It ain't nothing but a rag, but it's home to me. It's just something stuck together — I call it my shack. But I went to sleep hungry so many nights trying to pay for it — I don't know how many nights.

"And now they're fixing it up. This is just the most wonderful thing that ever happened to me."

The house seemed warmer, she said, even while the job was in progress. Before the men left, they also took time to solve a plumbing problem.

"They're people," Mrs. Green concluded. "Everybody makes mistakes. I'm praying for them."

The men returned at the end of each day to their three host families from the Trinity congregation — the Dimmocks, the Joyners, and the Hunters. Evenings and weekends were enjoyed together doing everything from playing basketball to shopping to just sitting and talking. One family took their guests to a college football game.

Said Harold West, Trinity's associate pastor, "Our people certainly had an opportunity to see the challenge for ministry — a ministry they could be part of with very little effort."

At our Wednesday family night, the six gave their Christian testmonies and fielded questions from the audience. Almost every member of the congregation was touched by the project through these public gatherings. It was another important step in our learning how to balance the social gospel with the individual gospel. No one could escape the point that what we do inside the church building is important, but what we do outside the building is equally important.

Six other churches helped us during those days. Volunteers from St. Mark's United Methodist and Longview Baptist provided lunches for the men. David Horner, pastor of Providence Baptist led some of the morning Bible studies. Members of his church provided some breakfasts, while others from Greenwood Forest Baptist helped with transportation.

Before returning to prison October 30, Bob Matters said, "This was one of the greatest experiences of my life. I praise the Lord for letting me get the furlough in order to do this. And I pray that public sentiment will make it possible for this kind of thing to become a permanent part of our justice system."

Bill Leffew, a retired contractor from Eden, North Carolina, who worked with the men, would agree with that. "I've been in the construction business for 30 years," he reflected, "and this is the best crew I ever had."

These two weeks opened two new windows for our church: practical ministry to the poor, and ministry to prisoners. We intend to do more of both in the future.

COUNSELING

Self-Service Disclosure

Counseling is a taxing ministry, no matter how many counselors share the load. Even with six full-time pastors, the staff at First Assembly of God in Grand Junction, Colorado, was swamped.

"One of the most time-consuming procedures is gathering initial information," says David Epps, minister of outreach and campus ministries. "We were spending lots of time tactfully asking the person about his or her background, spiritual awareness and commitment, previous history of problems, and so on."

Recently Epps streamlined this process by having counselees write down basic background information before they see the counselor. He uses the questions found in the Personal Data Inventory at the end of Jay Adams's *Competent to Counsel.*

Besides asking for name, address, health information, and religious background, the forms also ask:

- *What brings you here?*
- *What have you done about it?*
- *What can we do?*
- *Do you believe in God? Yes__ No__ Uncertain__.*
- *Do you pray? Never__ Occasionally__ Often__.*
- *Do you read the Bible? Never__ Occasionally__ Often__.*

Counselees are assured that all information will be kept confidential and that these facts are needed to help treat the problem.

"Most people offer no objection, and no one has refused to complete the questionnaire," says Epps.

"People can complete the forms in 15 minutes, rather than requiring one or two hours to get information through interviewing," says Epps. "In addition, many counselees for the first time are able to put down in black and white what troubles them, and that's therapeutic in itself."

Making the Most of Counseling Time

Steven C. Riser, associate pastor at Clairmont Presbyterian Church in the Atlanta suburb of Decatur, makes two simple requirements of those who want his counseling help:

1. In order to receive private ministry (counseling), you must also come regularly for public ministry (preaching and teaching).

2. In order to apply what is discussed in the session, you must complete the homework assignment before the next counseling appointment.

What if the person doesn't do the homework? That's not a problem, because Riser books the next appointment only *after* the homework has been done. "Call my secretary when you've finished doing this workbook," he will tell an engaged couple, "and she will be glad to set you up for our next time together." In this way, there's never an awkward confrontation with a person who has neglected to follow through.

"I try to show people my limitations as a counselor," Riser adds. "I can do very little if the person doesn't 'take the medicine' that's prescribed.

"The truth is, I'm probably doing less than half the counseling I would otherwise do, and with twice the results. People take the process seriously, because they see that we do more than sit and chat; we're about the business of Christian maturing."

To Charge
or Not to Charge

Alan H. Black, pastor of County Line Church of
God outside Auburn, Indiana, is willing to take
counselees from beyond his congregation, but he's
found that they participate more fully *if it costs* them
something.

"I see about a dozen outsiders each month," he says,
"and most of them expect to pay a fee." Yet Black feels
uneasy charging for what is essentially ministry.

His solution: "Only when I'm *asked* about a fee do I
tell the counselees, 'If, after a few sessions, you feel that
some progress is being made, you might wish to make
a tax-deductible contribution to the church and earmark
it for the pastor's professional library.' In most instances, this helps everyone feel comfortable."

About 80 percent do make contributions, ranging
from $10 to $40.

A Professional Next Door

When two different couples in Bethel Baptist
Church, Joliet, Illinois, were advised by local counselors
to proceed with divorce, Pastor Conrad Lundberg
knew something had to change. The nearest Christian
psychologist, however, was almost an hour away.

"We had several cases that went beyond my seminary counseling training," says Lundberg, "and I wanted
very badly to provide them with the help they
needed." The solution came when an associate pastor in
the area decided to move into full-time counseling
while he took additional studies.

"He needed office space and clients, so we worked

out an arrangement for him to work in our building every Friday. We provide an office, a car allowance, and some secretarial help. It's his practice, but in our facilities. He goes to two other towns on other days of the week."

About half the Joliet clients have turned out to be from Bethel, and another couple receiving help recently joined the church. "It's been good for us without incurring a lot of expense," the pastor says, "and it's been a boost for him."

A Missing Link in Counseling

When counselees with deep problems come to New Life Assembly of God in Yorkville, Illinois, they may see Pastor Paul Martin for only half the hour.

In some situations, they spend the first 30 minutes alone in the church's prayer room. "Go and cry out to the Lord everything you're going to tell me," Martin instructs them. "Lay it all before him — and then we'll come together to talk about what he has shown you in prayer."

Some are surprised by this approach, but so far no one has resisted or become angry. Many, of course, have never spent a full half hour praying about their difficulty. By the time they reach the pastor's office, their entire perspective is often changed.

"I was doing a lot of conventional counseling," Martin remembers, "and not seeing the changes I wanted to see. The Lord began speaking to me from the Psalms — the many times David says, 'I will call upon the Lord' and 'Pour out your heart before him' and 'Hear my cry, O Lord.' It struck me that the most profitable thing some people could do would be to tell God everything they were telling me, and wait for his responses.

"The effect has been incredible. Nearly all those who used to see me on a weekly basis have shown definite change. It has helped sort out those who are sincere, and it has hammered home the point that they don't come to *me* for answers, because I'm not the Source. They must come to the Lord with their problems."

This approach is not a gimmick to let Martin jam in twice as many appointments. "I don't have people stacked up like a doctor's office: one in the examining room and another waiting in the chair. No, while the counselee is in the prayer room, I'm praying and searching the Word in my office, too, preparing my heart and mind for the half hour we'll spend together. The focus becomes one of 'How will the Lord guide the two of us toward a solution to this problem?'"

Not every counseling situation warrants a half hour in prayer, of course. "I use this approach," Martin explains, "whenever I know in advance that the person has an especially deep need. And it's amazing what transpires."

Images That Heal

Howard Clinebell, professor of psychology at the School of Thelogy at Claremont in California, says that most people with religious backgrounds store away powerful images that can have a healing influence on a person's inner life.

Thus, in his counseling sessions Clinebell will sometimes ask, "Now, in your own words, why don't you tell me your favorite Bible story." This brings out of the person "living images" that obviously have some importance attached to them — otherwise they would have been forgotten.

If Clinebell hears the counselee reveal an image that might be therapeutic to whatever ailment he or she is experiencing, he may ask the person to meditate on that image, first in the counseling session and then later at home.

"If, for instance, I am counseling someone who feels bound emotionally, and the person vividly recalls the Old Testament story of the Jews' exodus from Egypt, I will suggest the person play the story through his mind, put himself into the action, and finally relate it to his own experience." Clinebell has seen more than one person helped to release from various sources of captivity by meditating on this image of deliverance.

The counselor remembers another time when, by recalling details of the story about the Prodigal Son, a person received healing strength for a problem that was a direct result of unresolved adolescent rebellion. The New Testament parables, the Cross, the Resurrection — each have provided healing images and symbols in Clinebell's counseling sessions.

"Of course, it's not the images that do the healing," Clinebell says, "but the images help people open up to the Holy Spirit."

Clinebell never prescribes a story, image, or symbol from his own experience, because "each image has to come out of the client's experience. A living symbol to me might be dead to someone else. The counselor's task is to help the client reach deep into his memory and recall his own meaningful images."

Learning from the Pros

The more marriages break up, the more pastors seek for ways to teach survival tactics, especially to engaged couples. A few years ago Dennis Kooy, minister of First Christian Church in Vale, Oregon, added some unique homework to his premarital counseling: interview someone who's been married 50 years.

"I require each bride to talk to an elderly wife and

each groom to talk to an elderly husband," says Kooy, who provides the following questions:
- *What has allowed your marriage to work?*
- *What have you personally done to help the marriage?*
- *How have you handled difficulties in your marriage?*
- *What have you done when the going got rough?*
- *As you look back over the last 50 years, what times were the hardest?*
- *What advice would you give to someone like me?*

"Nearly every young couple is scared to death at this assignment," reports Kooy, who has since moved to a church in Tillamook, Oregon. "They've never done an interview before. But when they come back, they're invariably excited. For many of them, it's the first time they've really studied a good pattern of marriage.

"They end up asking a lot of questions about the everyday things, especially money. Older people have some excellent things to say on that subject. Some of my counselees have even gone back on their own for a second visit."

Kooy insists on his requirement of 50 years or longer, even if it means sending the couple to a neighboring town. The elderly wife and the elderly husband do not necessarily have to be the spouses of each other, but both must still be married. And they enjoy the interview thoroughly. "Some have even called to thank me for the opportunity!" says Kooy.

"I've found that too many young couples searching for answers end up talking to other young couples just like themselves. This is a better way."

OUTSIDE ASSIGNMENTS IN PREMARITAL COUNSELING

by Donald L. Bubna, pastor, Salem Alliance Church, Salem, Oregon

Premarital counseling is time-consuming. Few couples realize or appreciate the time commitment of the officiating pastor to counseling sessions, rehearsal, rehearsal dinner, wedding ceremony, reception, and other involvements.

I have found that giving creative assignments to the couple promotes their own in-depth preparation for marriage and helps me save some time. These projects, done outside, make the actual counseling sessions much more effective. Here are six different assignments I've used.

1. *Paraphrase Ephesians 5:21-33.* I ask the couple to write separate paraphrases, encouraging them to enlarge, expand, and personalize the passage as much as they can without violating its meaning, as they understand it.

In the next counseling session, I ask them to read me their paraphrases. This ensures that they have worked through the basic scriptural principles about marriage, and it also provides a springboard for lively discussion about mutual submission and the roles of husband and wife.

2. *Be able to state in one or two sentences what you want your wedding to say.* While the real issue is the relationship, the wedding celebration is a public statement of the couple's beliefs about marriage. Forcing the couple to define their goals

for the service, in specific language, helps me understand what they want so I can help them plan their ceremony. It enables me to suggest how to include family members, how to use music to reflect their faith, and how to plan a wedding that is tasteful but not expensive. More importantly, hearing their goals for the wedding is a way to detect motivations and attitudes that may need to be dealt with before marriage.

3. *Write your own vows.* I remind the couple that marriage is based on commitment and that their ceremonial vows express the particulars of that. I suggest that they review several different vows but then write their own as lifelong promises to each other before God and their family and friends.

When the couple shows me their drafts during a counseling session, we review them and discuss the implications of these commitments.

4. *Do an in-depth interview with each of your families.* I ask them to make an appointment with their parents and thoughtfully ask, "What is it, Mom and Dad, that has made your marriage good?"

This strengthens family ties and helps transmit values from one generation to the next. Sometimes, when parents are divorced, couples have had to ask, "What can we learn from your experience to help make our marriage solid?"

Either way, their reporting session with me provides a good opportunity to discuss values and relationships with families.

5. *Develop a ninety-day budget.* Handling money is a problem in most marriages. The joint assignment of budget preparation forces the couple to discuss money matters and set priorities.

Frequently they resist this assignment, saying, "We don't know how much our income will actually be!" I persist, reminding them that their discipline now will prevent problems ahead.

When they bring their budget to me, I generally do not look at it but rather ask more general questions about spending habits, how they use a credit card, and what budget items would be cut back in a pinch.

6. *Visualize where you want to be in five years.* Many couples are happy with each other now, but they don't realize they're moving in different directions. This exercise helps the two people identify their individual goals. If these differ significantly, trouble could lie ahead.

For instance, in five years she wants to have three children, and he wants to have saved enough for a down payment on a house. Or, maybe she wants to finish college, and he wants to become the company's top salesman. Maybe he's unsure of his goals, and she's the one with definite ideas about the income level and type of neighborhood she expects in five years.

While none of these are necessarily incompatible goals, they may create pressure that the couple must be ready to handle.

Engaged couples can read many good books to supplement the counseling session. In addition, our church requires each couple to take a twelve-hour marriage preparation class. But I've found that assigning these outside projects is what brings a freshness to our counseling sessions, making them mutually enjoyable and profitable.

Today, a real Christian home is a miracle. Pastors who help couples build such homes can rejoice in their contribution to these brand-new family units as well as a strong new witness to the watching world.

Individual Group Therapy

Counseling has a built-in problem: if you focus on individuals, you have trouble seeing everyone as often as you should. But if you opt for group therapy, you can't always individualize the attention.

St. Andrew's Catholic Church in Fort Worth, Texas, has found a middle way.

"We have three groups that run concurrently for six weeks," says Diane Purcell, one of the group leaders. "Each group, however, is aimed at a specific kind of need."

Reach In helps participants deal with change, trauma, and struggles that come from within.

Reach Out concentrates on communication and dealing wtih the actions and feelings of other people.

Reach Up examines attitudes people have toward God.

"When a person comes to St. Andrew's for counseling," says Purcell, "we do an initial interview to determine the basic problem. Then we assign the person to one of the three groups. A mother who can't relate to her teenage son, for instance, we assign to Reach Out. A man who's angry at God for something in his past, we assign to Reach Up."

The groups meet for two hours twice a week. Each has six to eight participants and a trained group leader. Exercises and directed meditations based on gospel passages help the groups focus their discussions. Common topics include risk taking, feelings about fear, changing undesirable habits, and building self-esteem.

"Our people come because of divorces, alcohol in the family, career shifts, and change-of-life kinds of things," says Purcell.

"We've found that putting people of similar need together is an effective counseling method. It's exciting to watch people's attitudes change over six weeks as they realize they are not alone in the problem."

When to Stop Counseling

Robert L. Parsons, pastor of Centreville (Virginia) United Methodist Church outside Washington, has a self-imposed ceiling on the number of counseling sessions per person: no more than six.

"I try to explain in the first session that I am a pastor, not a psychotherapist," says Parsons. "I am glad to be a listener, a friend, and I will do what I do best — that is, give theological reflection on the difficulty the counselee is undergoing.

"I don't announce my cutoff point, of course, but I know in my own mind that if I am not able to help this person in six visits, then the problem is probably too critical for my skills, and I need to make a referral."

Parsons is in close touch with two professional pastoral counseling programs in the D.C. area and uses them readily.

What is the effect of such a strategy? "I'm probably a bit more directive in my counseling," he says, "since I know up front that I'm going to invest only a certain amount of time. I really try to speak from the theological stance, to bring out the biblical concepts that apply to the situation."

He remembers times in his early ministry when problems of transference and dependence grew after meeting with a person 15 or 20 times. Now, if someone clings to his counseling and resists being referred to someone else, Parsons kindly says, "I do want to help you, but I've given you about all I have to give at this point. It's time to broaden the input you're receiving."

FELLOWSHIP

Scrambled Eggs, Scrambled Ages

Sundays begin with a unique and popular 8:30 A.M. event at St. Andrews Presbyterian Church in rural Strathmore, California. Whole families — from toddlers to grandparents — breakfast together in the fellowship hall.

As many as 60 show up to eat, which is half the membership. The all-ages sharing seems to be the key to the breakfast's appeal. Children learn to converse as easily with a nonfamily adult as with their own parents.

"For 10 years we've watched the growth of our youth through these Sunday morning breakfasts," says Velma Zimmerman, church secretary. "We can see that they mature and gain social skills through the loving support of all ages in the congregation."

There are a few rules for the breakfasts. One or two couples sign up to cook; there is no special rotation. No reservations are required to attend.

The menu is always "cook's choice" and may be as simple as doughnuts and fruit. A favorite — biscuits and gravy — is the specialty of one man. The preparers arrive about 7:30, frequently bringing rolls, fruit, or juice ready to serve, leaving only coffee to be perked and eggs to be scrambled. Cooks are responsible for cleanup afterward, which is simplified by the use of disposable plates. Adults chip in $1 each; children 50¢.

After breakfast everyone applauds the cooks and joins in some singing before dividing into groups for Bible study. All ages come back together again to discuss the morning's lesson before adjourning to the sanctuary for worship.

Becky Burghardt, who joined St. Andrews six years ago, says, "I've taught Sunday school all my adult life, but I've never seen such community spirit and joyful inter-age sharing as our breakfasts generate."
Reported by Willma Gore

Blessings in a Bag

Potluck dinners are enjoyable for the eaters, but they can be a chore for the preparers. How do you keep the casseroles warm? And who gets stuck washing the dishes?

Grace Fellowship in Cahokia, Illinois, has eliminated such toil with "Brown Blessing Day." At least once a month following Sunday worship, the men re-arrange the folding chairs in the sanctuary, set up tables, and everyone breaks out a sack lunch.

"Before it's over," says Pastor Rick Kein, "people will inevitably share from one bag to another, which makes it practically a potluck — but without the hassle.

"We found that people were hanging around to talk long after the services were over, so we decided to let them eat while they were doing it," says Keim. "This way, no one has to rush off, and we don't have to worry about preparation or cleanup; it's a picnic-like atmosphere. The kids even seem to like it better when they can eat out of a bag."

Food for the Body and the Spirit

Congregations that eat together tend to stick around for the service that follows, it seems. Examples:

Wednesday Night Live is the rejuventated midweek program at First United Methodist Church in Ashland, Kentucky, and it all starts with a 6:30 meal.

"Our Wednesday night program has gone from 30 to 130 since we put together an exciting mix of six-week electives for all ages, preceded by a common supper," says Glenna Daut Fay, director of Christian education and leadership training. "We charge $2 per adult and $1 per child, up to $6 per family, and we always break even. Occasionally we even come out ahead."

At first the menu was soup and sandwiches, but that was too skimpy for the men. Now a full meat-and-potatoes fare is provided, prepared by a minister's widow in the church who's an excellent cook. She is paid for her work. One or two volunteers help her in the kitchen, while two or three others come early to set tables.

"The fellowship around the tables is great," reports Fay, "and at the end, we sing a song together and pray for those in the hospital. By 7:15 we're on our way to our sessions. The adults have three or four to choose from; there's a youth Bible study and a children's meeting as well."

Wednesday Night Live runs nine months a year, breaking only in the summer for home study groups.

Attendance picked up dramatically at Edgewater Baptist Church in Chicago, too, when a Wednesday night meal was provided one February. Here, a menu of homemade soup with bread, crackers, coffee, Kool-Aid, and cookies proved adequate. The prices: $1 for adults, 50¢ for children, and again no subsidy was required.

"We set up a rotation of four volunteer cooks," says Pastor William Hannaford. "One was a Jewish man who used to run a hot dog stand; he made a great kettle of chili. The other three were women who specialized in various kinds of soup."

Edgewater discontinued the meal at the beginning

of April, when interest seemed to wane. "It's a good thing for the short term," says Hannaford. "During the winter, people really like being able to drive straight from work, battle the snowy streets only once, and get inside for a warm bowl of soup with friends. Then in the spring, it seemed less appealing.

"We're going to try it again now this summer, only we'll change to salad and fixings as the temperature goes up and the lettuce prices come down."

The meal was followed at 7:15 by kids' clubs, prayer meeting, and choir rehearsal.

At another urban church, First Alliance in New York City, a Sunday noon meal is "the main fellowship event of our church," says Pastor Eugene McGee. He started the all-church lunch almost accidentally one week when he happened upon a chow mein bargain at a wholesale food outlet. He bought a large quantity, added some chickens, and whipped the dinner together himself. About 20 people stayed to eat it. "Splitting the cost, it came to about 35 cents each," he remembers.

The meal turned out to be the ideal spacer in the church's newly consolidated schedule. McGee and his board had found that the traditional evening format was a problem in Manhattan; people feared being out at night and disliked making two crosstown trips in one day. So the new schedule was:

9:30	Early Sunday school
11:00	Worship
12:00	Common meal
2:00	Late Sunday school
3:00	"Evening church"

The lunch crowd has grown, and not only for reasons of convenience. "One of the biggest reasons inner-city churches die is lack of a social life," McGee explains. "People come to First Alliance from all five boroughs, and this is their one opportunity to get to know and reach out to each other."

Huxley, Iowa, is a long way from New York City, both in miles and lifestyle. But at the Berean Baptist Church, they too believe in the advantages of a preservice meal.

"We used to have our carry-in dinners after the morning service," says head deacon Bob Niehoff, "but there was always the problem of keeping food fresh and warm for several hours during Sunday school and church.

"Now we have the dinners an hour before the evening service instead. It gives the ladies a lot more flexibility in what they can bring. Everyone arrives fresh and relaxed, with food piping hot, ready to be served."

Unlike the others, this church does not have a weekly meal. But the benefits of fellowship across the table are valued here as well, and the evening service receives the extra impetus.

Dinners for Six

Here are two modern examples of the New Testament practice of "breaking bread from house to house . . . with gladness" (Acts 2:46).

About every five weeks, 80 to 85 percent of the adults in the Free Methodist Church, Lawrence, Kansas, have dinner together. One guest couple brings the salad and another brings the dessert; the host couple furnishes the entree.

The dinners are scheduled for Friday or Saturday nights alternately. Dates are posted for three dinners at a time, and members sign up either as hosts or guests. From these sheets, coordinator Darlene Atkinson makes the assignments in groupings of six.

"I keep a record and try to keep matching guests and hosts who have not been together at previous dinners," she says. "I mix age groups and people with varied social, economic, and eduational backgrounds. By rotating, married couples serve as hosts only every three months, and singles every six months."

Almost all the regular single adults in the church participate, often in pairs. Currently about 15 to 20 University of Kansas students are involved.

x

"If I run short of hosts," says Atkinson, "I have a few names in reserve who have said they'll serve as hosts anytime."

The church, which has an average Sunday morning attendance of 260, has had Dinners for Six for more than four years. Results, according to Atkinson:

- People have learned to know each other on a more intimate level.
- The dinners have broken down age and educational barriers.
- They've established a background for more meaningful conversations at church.
- They've resulted in some close relationships.

After one recent dinner, a guest suffered a severe asthma attack. The hostess, a nurse, recognized the seriousness of the illness, called an ambulance, and she immediately began CPR treatment along with her daughter.

As a result of the incident, one of the medics offered to teach a CPR course at the church without charge. Forty people enrolled.

"We always pray before we place people at these dinners," Atkinson says. "I believe God especially answered in this case."

Reported by Ruth Richert Jones

At Clearlake Baptist Church in the northern California town of Lakeport, groups stay together for a three-month period, making the rounds of each home in turn.

The groups are randomly matched up at all-church potlucks held in January, May and September. Each family jots its name on a slip of paper and drops it in a box at the door. At the end of the evening, names are drawn in groups of three.

Each group then assembles to decide who will host the others on which night over the next three months. On the fourth month, another all-church potluck is held, and new groups are chosen.

Each dinner includes a devotional given by the hosting family. Each group is also assigned to pray for a specific church-supported missionary.
Reported by Marilyn Wilcox

The No-Hassle Guest List

"If we invite the Schmidts and Renellas over after church, will the Murphys be upset at not being included?" Pastors and their spouses may wish they didn't have to worry about such minutiae, but such are the social facts of church life.

Gary and April Bowman, who serve the Evangelical Free Church of Chula Vista, California, have a unique way to entertain regularly without hurting anyone's feelings. Over a year's time, they hosted five anniversary parties in their home — one for couples married in each season of the year, plus an extra night just for June.

"We averaged about ten couples each time," says Gary, "and it was great. April always served her famous Mud Pie" (a chocolate lover's ecstasy), "we played some games, and we went around the circle sharing 'Here's what's right with my spouse.'"

Some of the advantages:

• Couples were mixed in new groupings.

• The event had some advance suspense, since no one was quite sure who else would be coming.

• More than two thirds of the church's adults got to be in the pastor's home.

• Marital relationships were strengthened.

"The last group, October-December, was small anyway, so we threw it open to any who had missed earlier due to illness, travel, or whatever," Gary explains.

"We're about to begin a second round of anniversary parties, because we think it's a creative, fun way to organize fellowship."

For larger congregations: Schedule the parties by month instead of season.

A Pumped-up Party

When the young-couples class at Stevens Point Assembly of God in Wisconsin held its "Fall Harvest Party," no one could say it came as a surprise.

That's because the first announcement went out in April.

"We sent everyone a letter with two or three pumpkin seeds in the envelope," says Sandi Lindberg, pastor's wife. "We asked couples to grow pumpkins in their back yards to bring to the fall event. This plant was a reminder all summer of a special time to come."

Class members chatted often as the months went by about how their crop was coming, how to defend against squirrels, chickens, and other scavengers, and who would win the prize for the largest pumpkin.

The group, which averages 20 on Sunday morning, swelled to twice that number when the night finally came. More than half arrived carrrying the results of their labors. "We encouraged everyone to dress country or western and bring something like apple or pumpkin pie, fried chicken, or cider to share," says Lindberg. The evening's festivities included awards (calico-wrapped soaps, homemade jams or breads) for the largest and the tiniest pumpkins. They also decorated pumpkins with construction paper, glue, and markers to make faces.

"The point of all the fun, of course," the Lindbergs

add, "was to strengthen the class as a group, help us get closer to the young couples in our church, and intertwine those who enjoy Sunday morning with those who come only occasionally."

Invite-a-Member-to-Dinner Sunday

Once every year the families of Olivet Evangelical Congregational Church, Bethlehem, Pennsylvania, pair up for a Sunday dinner.

An announcement is made about three weeks ahead of time, and a sheet with all church members is placed on the church bulletin board.

When a family invites another family (or families), they check each name off the list. Some families will invite a group of singles, young people, or senior citizens.

"We specifically ask," says William J. McEllroy, Jr., pastor, "that people invite those whom they are not well acquainted with. It's a time of getting to know new faces." Creative fellowship is encouraged. One family invited a group of senior adults and taught them to play Flinch, the popular card game, after dinner.

Some families go home together right after the Sunday morning service; others plan their dinner for later in the day. "The idea," says McEllroy, "is for the fellowship to carry though the entire afternoon so the families can go together to the evening service. Usually we plan a special activity, such as a family film."

McEllroy says it's a great idea, not just for the members but for the pastor's family too. "My three young children have been shown that we can take part in the friendships of other families in the church," he adds.

The program has proven successful through the years. McEllroy illustrates:

"One young family had a baby that had been born two months premature. Under this anguish, they wound up having Sunday dinner with another young family with several children. The women liked each other immediately.

"Two months passed, with the baby still in the hospital and not expected to live, and the parents continued under pressure and uncertainty. But the new family stayed in close touch and, with the Lord's help, pulled them through the crisis. The two families are signed up to be cosuperintendents of this year's Vacation Bible School."

King-Sized Compliment

It's one thing to affirm the congregation from the pulpit, but it's quite another to let the whole world know.

During Pastor Louis Konopka's first five months at Blythefield Hills Baptist Church, Rockford, Michigan, he emphasized unity and love for one another by preaching through Ephesians and James. Then he decided to take his own messages to heart by renting a billboard at a nearby intersection, close to two restaurants frequented by church people. There he proclaimed: *The people at Blythefield Hills Baptist Church are the GREATEST!* (Signed) *Pastor*.

The sign was up for two weeks. Not a word was said in the services except for a passing joke by one evening song leader. But the sign caused plenty of buzzing and smiling in the narthex and hallways. Even the Gannett Sign Company, which had originally quoted a price of $500, was impressed. In the end, they decided not to bill the job at all.

Reported by Ruth Smith

Honoring the Unsung

Every church has its unsung heroes. At Windsor Hills Baptist Church in La Mesa, California, Ruth Raush is one of the inconspicuous faithful.

"She's forever giving of herself to the church," says deacon chairman Frank Andrews. "Every Sunday she brings flowers from her garden for the altar and bags of fruit from her trees for anyone who wants it. She notices whenever anyone is sick and sends a card. She's a widow and in her eighties, but she's as active as ever, a Sunday school teacher, a deaconess, and responsible for the Communion elements.

"And in all these years, I don't know if anyone had ever thanked her."

So Andrews and the Windsor Hills congregation recently staged a "Ruth Raush Appreciation Day."

"Sunday morning attendance was the biggest we've had in years," says Andrews. "Many members who'd moved away came back for the occasion."

Everything, of course, was a surprise for Ruth. Pastor Terry Miller read a biographical tribute, and she was given a corsage and an autograph book with thank-you notes from all the church members. Her son, daughter-in-law, and grandchildren, who live in a neighboring town, came for the event, and Ruth was the guest of honor at the afternoon potluck.

"We figured it's best to honor people while they're still active and part of the church," says Andrews. "This event was such a success that the deacons voted to have official recognition days like this twice a year."

Encouragement Sunday

Twice a year at Cedarville Community Church in Indiana, the entire congregation takes time to practice 1 Thessalonians 5:11 — "Therefore encourage one another and build each other up."

A Sunday morning handout sheet asks everyone — including visitors — to tear off the bottom portion and fill in name, address, and phone. After folding the paper once and putting it in the offering plates when passed specifically for that purpose, people receive the plates a second time. Each person draws out a friend to encourage secretly in the coming week.

"Most people find this to be a very uplifting experience," says Pastor Les Martin. "Receiving a card, book, cassette, or bakery items is nice, but the giving is even greater. It generates a lot of enthusiasm."

One woman set her home-baked pie on a porch, rang the doorbell, and ran away — only to be chased by the recipient's dog. Fortunately, the person came to the door before the dog could return to devour the pie.

A man in his 70s, fearful that his handwriting would give away his identity, went to the bother of cutting out newspaper words and letters and pasting them onto a homemade card to send.

"We do this every March and November," says the pastor, "and even visitors participate. We take time the following Sunday morning for reports of how various people were encouraged."

Some of the stories are funny, but others come from those like the man who had been working in his garage on a balky water softener. He had already paid for one expensive repair call, but now the machine had clogged again. "I was really getting discouraged," he said, "when just then, the doorbell rang. I laid down my wrench to go see who was there — and found this huge card: 'When things are going bad, just remember someone's thinking about you.' It was a message I really needed at that moment."

Sowing a Crop of Compliments

Despite the folksy saying that "It's easier to catch flies with honey than vinegar," most people find it harder to compliment than criticize.

Giving and receiving words of encouragement are skills worth developing. Two churches have tried to make the practice habit-forming.

For several years the Church of Christ in North Bend Oregon, has had a bulletin board filled with "Flowers for the Living" — notes of encouragement from one member to another. Cards (puchased and homemade), stationery, and often just scraps of paper are used to convey gratitude, congratulations, or sympathy.

"Fred, thanks for your faithful work in the bus ministry."

"Congratulations on your graduation, Carol; we're proud of you."

"I heard you've been going through some deep water, Scott. Hang in there. I'm praying for you."

More personal words are often put into a sealed envelope with the recipient's name on the outside and tacked to the board.

The idea is kept alive by occasional mention from the pulpit, and the two ministers lead the way in putting up a few notes each week. "But we've found the board doesn't need much promotion," says Mark McLean. "It carries its own momentum."

Teens use the board to display birthday greetings. Sunday school classes pass along cards on wedding anniversaries.

"Although the board has been used several years, members are eager to see if they have a message," says McLean. "The board has been helpful in building up the body of Christ."

The second Sunday of each month is "Encouragement Sunday" at First United Presbyterian Church in Moline, Illinois. Postcards are provided in the pew racks, and during announcements, people are invited to write notes of encouragement to someone who's sick, a shut-in, a Sunday school teacher — anyone who comes to mind.

Cards are then placed in the offering plate. On Monday the church secretary and the outreach committee address the cards and mail them, usually 50 to 60 cards each month.

Reported by George Kalemkarian

Year-Round Cheer

Christmas may not be the best time to send greeting cards after all. Pastor Ralph Klassen avoids the rush and sends a personal letter to each of the couples in his church on their wedding anniversary. At Lakeview Mennonite Brethren Church in Lethbridge, Alberta, that amounts to 45 or 50 letters a year, "and dozens of those are in June and July," says Klassen.

"I do it for several reasons. It lets people know I care. I remember them specifically. And it emphasizes the value of good marriages and Christian homes."

Klassen usually includes a Scripture verse appropriate for each family and tells the couple why he appreciates them.

Response, he says, has been great.

"Thanks for your personal contact," said one couple.

"We don't have any children living nearby anymore," said another couple. "It's nice to have someone here remember this special occasion. Are you and your wife free to come over for dinner to celebrate?"

Postal Prayers

When Mount Franklin Baptist Church prays, the words aren't spoken heavenward and forgotten. For the price of a postage stamp, the El Paso, Texas, church also sends a message to the person needing prayer.

The church uses six different "concern cards" for various situations: hospitalization, graduation, a birth, a death, or serious illness. During Wednesday night prayer neeting, the pastor discusses the current needs and asks if anyone else has a request. Then concern cards are distributed for each personal request, and people sign their names with a brief word of encouragement.

"We'll mail a card to anyone, anywhere — if someone wants us to," says Bob White, minister of education. From three to twelve cards may be distributed on any given Wednesday.

The colorful 8½-by-11 notes are printed on stiff card stock with an artistic border, the name of the church, a caption, and plenty of space for personal messages.

The various captions read: "In Deepest Sympathy," "We Rejoice in Your Recovery," "You're Something Beautiful," "We Rejoice in Your Happiness," "We're Praying for You" (for short-term illness), and "We Love and Pray for You" (for long-term illness).

"Recently the sister of a woman in our congregation was hospitalized for a chemical dependency problem," says White. "We sent her a card, and she wrote back to say, 'Thanks for not giving up on me.' Even though she'd never been to the church, she knew we cared."

Push-Button Visitation

How can the whole church family send greetings to
- shut-ins?
- members who are hospitalized?
- missionaries overseas?

The Alhambra Seventh-day Adventist Church in California wanted to do more than mail a card from the church office. Their solution? A 90-minute cassette filled with two-minute greetings from members of the congregation.

"Maybe 12 times in the past four months," says Pastor Gayland Richardson,"we've set up an easel in the foyer with a sign inviting people to say hi to a certain member of the congregation."

Below the sign is listed some information about the member who cannot attend the worship service. A volunteer recruits passers-by to tape their greetings and helps those unfamiliar with the portable recorder.

"One time, for instance, our long-time custodian was in intensive care," says Richardson. "It was impossible for most to visit him personally, but we filled a cassette with people sharing a verse of Scripture and telling him they were praying for him."

When Bruce and Linda Bauer, missionaries in Osaka, Japan, received their cassette, they were so moved they recorded a greeting of their own and sent it to the church: "We cried when we got your tape. You don't know how good it is to hear voices from home."

Richardson admits, "It's nothing elaborate, but it lets people communicate in ways that go beyond a card or phone call from the pastor."

Pastoral Visits: What to Talk About

Calling on the membership is a venerable tradition, but many pastors have stopped their stopping by. A frequent reason: they feel awkward to force a visit without a pretext or invitation. Conversation seems strained, and aren't families too busy these days anyway?

Phil Blake doesn't buy that argument. He designed a short icebreaker questionnaire that he mails to the home a couple of weeks ahead. The adults fill it out and have it ready when the doorbell rings; it becomes a natural starting point.

The questions, adapted from the Quaker Dialogue, are:

1. *Where were you born?*
2. *When you were young, how did you heat your home?*
3. *How long have you lived here?*
4. *What person has influenced your life the most?*
5. *What made you decide to worship at this church?*

"It relieves people's anxiety and gets us going." says Blake, who has built a Families in Focus program around it. "Sometimes I think churches work so hard to accommodate the new folk that the old-timers can get to wondering, 'Don't we count, too?'"

The other elements of Families in Focus are:

• A cover letter with the questionnaire that says the family will be one of four or five who are featured the week of ___, unless they have a conflict of some kind.

• Their names are listed in the Sunday bulletin, and they're introduced in the morning service by having them stand.

• Pastor Blake nails down the hour for his visit at the door as the family leaves the service. "I suggest a time, and people generally try very hard to accommodate; they're pleased that I want to be with them in their homes," he says.

During his 13 years at Big Lake Church of God in Columbia City, Indiana, he worked through the membership three different times. When he went to the larger West Washington Street Church of God in Indianapolis, he managed to visit all but seven or eight of the 200 member families.

"It gets to be exciting," Blake adds, "as families and households look forward to their turn to be a Family in Focus."

They Don't Miss This Bulletin Board

Southside Baptist Church in the county seat town of Cochran, Georgia, has solved the problem of people ignoring the church bulletin board.

Each Sunday morning there's a new mystery picture on the board: a baby or childhood shot of one of the members. Below is a sheet for guessing who the person is. The winners are announced in the church newsletter that goes out by mail late in the week.

"This was the brainstorm of our Royal Ambassador Boys," explains Pastor Hubert Addleton, referring to the teen boys' club. "They have a great time going around collecting old pictures. They started out with a baby picture of me the first week, which stumped everyone — nobody guessed me. Since then, they've had a new picture every week, and now they're even doing two a week.

"It makes for a lot of fun, especially when they post what turns out to be a dignified deacon or other church leader. But best of all, it gets everyone to stop by and notice the announcements, posters, and various sign-up sheets on the rest of the bulletin board."

The boys and their leader show up early each Sunday to mount the mystery picture on an attractive background and prepare a new sheet that says "My Guess" and "My Name." Guessing continues all day Sunday and on Wednesday night as well, after which the boys reveal to Addleton the true identity and the correct guesser(s), if any. "Then, of course, this gives me a way to get more members' names into the newsletter," the pastor adds, "which is always a good idea."

Circles Yes, Cliques No

When the suggestion came from headquarters back in the 1950s that women's circles ought to be scrambled every so often, the ladies of Erwin United Methodist Church in Syracuse, New York, were not impressed. They promptly voted it down.

A few years later, the subject came up again, with stronger emphasis this time, and the proposal passed. Members would be reassigned to a new circle every two years in order to get to know more women and keep all the circles from stagnating.

Some still didn't like it. A few stopped going to their assigned circles, and one woman left the church altogether. But the others were gradually won over, and after 20 years, the practice is a solid tradition at Erwin Church.

"Every other fall, a committee of members from all the circles works on the list and mixes up the names," explains Marion Rush. "We try to create a balance in each group of young and older, shut-in and active, drivers and nondrivers. This way no circle is ever allowed to grow so elderly that it becomes inactive; new life is regularly being introduced.

"At our January luncheon, we sit at tables according to the new groupings. Each new circle elects its officers after lunch and decides its meeting places for the coming months.

"The result is that we become well acquainted with more clusters of new people while still retaining our friendships throughout the larger group."

Anybody Need a Toaster?

When people go to the annual rummage sale at Grace Baptist Church, Racine, Wisconsin, they leave their money home. They don't need it.

"Exchange Day," as it is called, is basically a giant garage sale each June at which everything is free. As Jane Worsham, the pastor's wife, explains, "We simply aim to provide a little structure to stimulate a lot of sharing within the church body."

On the day for bringing items, members stream into the fellowship hall with pots, pans, dishes, wall hangings, baby equipment, all sizes of clothing, toys, games, books, and electrical appliances. The only requirements are that the items must be clean and in good repair.

The same people then return on Exchange Day to pick up anything they would like. Since they are fellow Christians who have to keep worshiping with one another in the future, they don't succumb to the fierce elbowing that sometimes occurs at regular garage sales. "We see it as a chance to share our discards with others who can use them," says Worsham. "This opportunity to give or receive within the fellowship is an expression of our love for one another."
Reported by Fran Adams

A similar idea thrives at Omega Fellowship in Santa Ana, California — but on a year-round basis. A large "Share Table" is available for people to give and receive whenever the church is open. "Children's clothing, homemade food, and knickknacks are the most common items," says Barbara L. McGraw, minister at Omega.

"Our only rule is that they must be in excellent condition; we believe in giving away the first fruits," she adds. "There's no supervision or record keeping; anybody in need is welcome.

"Surprisingly, in the six years we've done this, the table has always been full."

The Hospitality Basket

In an adult class at Trinity Presbyterian Church in Montgomery, Alabama, the hospitality chairman showed up one morning carrying an empty basket. A red bow was tied to the top.

"This basket represents an invitation to fellowship here in our group," he announced to the eight or ten couples. Handing the basket to one of them, he continued, "We'd like to have you come to our house one night this week for pie and coffee. I'll call you later to pick a day and time. Then next week, or as soon as possible, you can bring the basket and invite another couple to your home."

The basket moved through the group over the next few months, eventually reaching everyone, since no one was to accept more than one invitation during the program. Each Sunday morning, the class leader asked who had the basket and made sure it was moving along. "If you invite someone for more than just dessert," he added, "keep it simple. We want to emphasize hospitality and not entertainment. This is a basket, not a silver tray."

The class members thoroughly enjoyed this simple method of getting together. As one person said, "It helped us turn our good intentions into action."
Reported by Sara Ann DuBose

STEWARDSHIP MEANS MORE THAN $ $ $

by Charles R. Birner, pastor, Abiding Savior Lutheran Church, El Toro, California

When pastors talk about "time, talents, and treasure" in a stewardship campaign, you can usually translate that with one word — *money.* For years I was determined to find a way to emphasize more than that. Then in the spring of 1982 I came up with the idea of a "Glory to God Festival."

"What's a 'Glory to God Festival'?" asked Jim, chairman of our board of lay ministry.

"It's a chance for people to give of their time, talents, and treasures — period. No asking for money the whole day. We'll simply let people show the gifts God has given them — and give God the glory for it."

After the board approved the idea, the work began.

There were many questions to be answered. "Will it be like a bazaar?" "Will we have food?" "Will we allow people to sell their products?" "If we do, will some of the money go to the treasury?"

I answered the questions as best I could. I suggested a Saturday in November, our normal month for stewardship emphasis. I wanted people to see that in preparing for the festival they were giving the Lord their *time,* that the skill they invested meant giving their *talents,* and the finished goods represented their *treasures.* Nothing would be for sale — only for admiration.

Then, on the following Sunday, we could proceed with our usual gathering of financial pledges.

As the concept became clear, the details came together. Charlotte Meyer began scheduling the church's various music groups. Verna Heckman developed some skits and readings for adults in our congregation. Marion Wuertz started to recruit people with special skills in arts and crafts such as pottery, stained glass, and woodworking.

We knew we had to start early, before summer vacations hit. Shirley Hess developed Sunday bulletin inserts that told about the "Glory to God Festival" to be held in November. At the end she put an enrollment form that asked for name, address, phone number, and talents to be displayed. We primed the pump by including a long list of different talent possibilities — since many people overlook their most obvious abilities.

We held one more meeting before summer, deciding to have an evening meal at the festival. Everyone agreed Perry Chamberlain excelled in this department, so the call went out to him.

"How many people are you talking about?" asked Perry. Our optimism showed when we told him maybe a couple hundred.

Summer months rushed by; the entire project seemed to lie dormant. But with the return of vacationing families, life emerged. Minds had not slept during vacation. It was time for detailed planning.

I admit I don't have the gifts to orchestrate big events. Carolyn Sims and Barbara Lapinski, cochairpersons, knew this. So they had already singled out Don Rehder to handle that chore. He had people signing participation sheets and assured us that everything would indeed happen between 2:00 and 8:00 on November 20. We trusted him.

Friday night before the big day, tables were placed ready for exhibits, and spots were marked on the floor for those who planned to bring their own display materials. Displays filled the back of the gym; others were lined up along the side walls. The total list came to 53 exhibits.

Saturday arrived, and everything went beautifully. The gym was filled with handicrafts, knitting, needlepoint, woodworking, clocks, cross-stitch, oil paintings, crochet, doll collections, and beautiful stained-glass windows of various shapes. Gary Jurgemeyer, teacher of pottery at Laguna Hills High, brought his potter's wheel and made items as people watched. Even a go kart found its way to a stand — "It'll go 70 miles an hour," Conrad assured us. There were no takers.

People walked among the displays. The crowd kept building as the afternoon hours passed. At regular intervals during the six-hour period, musical and drama groups gave presentations at one end of the gym. That way, people could walk around for a while, then sit for a performance as they caught their breath, then move on to other displays.

The musical groups were great. Associate Pastor Jim Kuntz did his infamous Victor Borge sketch. Other selections ran from "Praise the Lord! O Heavens Adore Him!" by our school choir to a Puccini aria to "Star Wars" on the piano to a command performance by "Uncle Charlie (me) and the Sunshine Boys" (four other men of the church).

At 5:30 a chili supper was served to about 300 people. It was the perfect informal menu, and people wandered about eating and talking until 7:00. We ended the day with a serious drama presentation, a short devotional I had prepared, and the quiet singing of "In our lives, Lord, be glorified."

By 8:30 the crowd began a homeward trek, people packed up their displays, and cleanup began. Comments as they departed were gratifying: "I thought I knew these people. I found out a lot more about them as I spoke with them about their gifts." "I thought the paintings had to be religious — otherwise I could have brought mine."

The results went beyond a deepened awareness of others' gifts, though. Dennis was a reluctant participant because he thought his talents were too "hobbyish." Still, he put his work on display.

"I received many nice comments, and it made me feel close to those with similar gifts," he said later. "But the real value for me was in realizing I could help others by showing a similar interest in their gifts. I invited a friend with marriage difficulties to work with me on model airplanes, a common hobby. The friend has now been worshiping with us and is interested in finding out more about this Christian faith. It never ceases to amaze me how God works with something as mundane as a yellow model glider."

We're planning a festival for next year. People know what to expect now and have been suggesting new ideas to incorporate. Two times in a row may be enough, though. We think a "Glory to God Festival" should be an every-now-and-then thing, a spontaneous burst of thanks to God for our special gifts and the opportunity to share them with Christian brothers and sisters.

When Members Move Away: A Consolation

In a mobile society, there's simply no stopping the exodus of members to other parts of the country. The only thing you *can* control, says Donnie Whitney, pastor of Glenfield Baptist Church outside Chicago, is your attitude about the transfers.

Instead of bemoaning the losses, this suburban church has decided to be positive about the people it has sent elsewhere in the Kingdom. The women's mission group created a patchwork map display, using bright scraps of cloth cut into the shapes of the 50 states. After researching where former members had moved to, they drew up lists by states and attached thin ribbons from Glenfield's location to the various states represented. The members' names were also posted on or nearby the states.

"Now instead of regretting the loss of so many fine members," says Whitney, "the map helps us see how our church has affected the lives of people all over America. We update the lists quarterly."

Many churches use world maps to show where their missionaries are serving, but the U.S.A. map helps us remember that we're *all* on mission and that our church is a missions training base," says the pastor.

GOOD MOURNING

by Helen G. Taylor, minister, Leland Clegg Memorial United Methodist Church, Oklahoma City, Oklahoma

Funerals are never welcome in a church's life, especially when a member dies in the summer of his years. But when we shared the grief of Jerry Armstrong's family, we found our lives profoundly touched.

Jerry, 42, died of a sudden heart attack after his regular evening jog one Monday night in October 1981. Amid the shock and grief of the next few hours, several of us, his close friends, gathered in his home with his widow, Karen, and their two teenage daughters, Sherrie and Michelle. We began to discuss plans.

Karen was very clear about two points. First, she didn't want a "commercial" funeral. She and Jerry had for years practiced simple living, helping our church begin a work co-op to share labor and a produce co-op to reduce food costs. And they had been deeply involved in a three-month "Death and Dying" series in our adult Sunday school. Karen and the girls wanted no fancy casket — just a simple pine box and a quilt.

Second, Karen knew this event would touch the whole community of faith, and she wanted to involve everyone who wanted to help.

As the details were quickly worked out, over 30 of the people in our church of 100 active members became involved. It did indeed become a project for the whole church. David Shelden, a layman and Jerry's tennis buddy, volunteered to coordinate the effort.

Tuesday morning, David, Karen, my husband, and I went to look for a burial site. Out in the country north of Oklahoma City, we came to a cemetery on a gentle slope. There we found a grassy spot in the shade of a blackjack oak with a couple of fat mushrooms growing nearby. We exchanged smiles with the settled feeling that, yes, here was the right place. A lone bird trill broke the quiet of the walk back to the car.

That afteroon 12 men in work clothes gathered in a garage and studied the dimensions of a casket sketched on typing paper. After discussing measurements, they began the sawing, nailing, and sanding.

In the meantime, one of the newer members of the church donated her own hand-stitched quilt with a double-wedding-ring pattern. She and some friends took the quilt to Jerry's friends so they could write farewell messages with felt-tip pen on the underside. One wrote a short poem on the fabric.

In another house, a group of women created a banner out of red wool, stitching and gluing designs symbolic of Jerry's active outdoor life: a motorcycle helmet, a canoe, a silhouette of the family, a bow and arrows. It read simply, "Jerry Armstrong, 1939-1981."

Another group prepared the church building, scrubbing floors, hauling chairs, and rearranging furniture. They also handled the stream of food, flowers, and phone calls that poured in.

In two days the work was done. The men had a lovely pine coffin with routed moulding around the brass handles on either side. The lid was beveled with a cross built in and lightly stained so it looked like honeyed ivory. The homemade coffin was sturdy, weighing almost 200 pounds empty.

Early Thursday morning, before the funeral service, the banner was hung at the front of the church, and the coffin was taken to the funeral home. Six friends, serving as pallbearers, brought the body back to the church and placed it in the sanctuary (resting on two Workmate benches draped with dark tablecloths).

Church people arranged the flowers, made and tended the guest book, ushered, and directed traffic for a crowd twice the church's capacity.

The worship service itself began with two friends closing the casket, and then David Shelden gave an original call to celebration: "As an athlete practices and practices to become better and better, a community of faith must practice and practice to become strong. We practice by eating together, dancing together, crying together, and laughing together."

The service moved through congregational hymns, prayer, Scripture readings, and then I preached on the "green pastures" of Psalm 23 — the outdoors where Jerry had often said he felt closest to God. I recalled that just two weeks before his death, Jerry had preached in our church. He talked about his heart by-pass surgery six years earlier and the terror he'd felt during that crisis.

"Even when my heart stopped that first time," he had said, "I knew God was there. I don't know what lies ahead for me, but I know that in God's world, it will be good."

At one point in the service, we gave opportunity for anyone to share a brief word about Jerry. We experienced both laughter and tears.

A neighbor who had also had by-pass surgery said, "Jerry and I didn't have much time to talk. But I often saw him as he jogged and I walked. I'll always remember the way he greeted me and the touch of his hand."

We also sang "Amazing Grace," and never have I heard it sung with such deep meaning.

The service ended with everyone singing "Shalom" and holding hands in a circle that included the coffin. In the singing, the sharing, the doing — the overflow crowd, many of whom were strangers, became a community.

We sensed it even more as the coffin was placed in a

station wagon and driven by friends to the gravesite. There by the blackjack oak we had a short service. Two hours later friends and family returned with their own shovels to cover the grave. It was a moving good-by, far more friendly than being buried by a machine — or strangers.

Yes, it was an unusual celebration by today's standards. But it's really an old way — and a good way — of dealing with the pain of death.

There are legal restrictions. We made sure to consult a lawyer before proceeding, because the laws vary from state to state. The only thing Oklahoma required was that the body, if not buried within 24 hours of death, be either embalmed or refrigerated.

Other than that, we discussed what we wanted with the funeral home and vault company, and they were very cooperative.

This has been a life-changing event for us all, individually and as a congregation. In working together, there was an honesty in looking at death that diminished the horror and helped all of us face it with more strength. In the process, we also worked out a lot of grief and worked in a sense of community.

When death is dealt with so openly, and the experience is shared by the church, it really does lose its sting — in victory!

OLDER ADULTS

Sunday Grannies

More older women wouldn't mind helping in the church nursery if it didn't exhaust them for the rest of the day. Rocking a baby is a delight, but all that changing and chasing of toddlers overdoes it.

That's why St. Mary's-on-the-Highlands Episcopal Church in Birmingham created a special rank of nursery personnel: the Rocking Chair Guild. Their only job is to rock, love, and lullaby babies. The rest of the work is done by a paid supervisor and a volunteer aide.

Sara Larson, who organizes the half-dozen women on a rotation, found them timid at first but soon in love with the job. "Some of them live far from their own grandchildren, and this gives them the chance to cuddle the little ones.

"One of our ladies, Jean Voight, got a special delight in the grocery store one day when a child from the church ran up to her and said, 'Hi, Granny!'"
Reported by Claire Bouton

A Crew for You

If you don't know what a *bubbler* is, you probably don't live in irrigation country. But if you decide to retire in a place like Sun City, Arizona, you'll find out soon enough. Bubblers are lawn watering systems, and they need adjustment from time to time.

That's where the Handymen of Faith United Presbyterian Church come in.

"Sun City is a planned community of 48,000 people, all over 50 years of age," Associate Pastor Wilson

Yost explains. "That means we have numbers of widows and others who need help maintaining their houses or duplexes. For the past eight years, the Handymen have been organized to respond."

The current roster includes 35 men and 1 woman who fix everything from bubblers to plumbing to drapery to garage doors. They also help with income tax, Medicare claims, wills and trusts, and life insurance. Several of the Handymen specialize in cost estimating: when a job is too complex for amateurs, they guide the homeowner in getting bids from repair firms and choosing the best one. The group maintains a list of recommended service companies.

"Last year we made 72 different minor repairs and 34 referrals," says Bill Holman, a retired steel company president who now chairs the Handymen, taking calls and dispatching members to help. "Most of us aren't what you'd call lifelong craftsmen; a town like Sun City attracts more professional types — engineers, educators, doctors, attorneys. So if the job turns out to be too big for us, we say so. But we enjoy seeing what we can conquer."

The Handymen make no charge for their service other than the cost of the parts and occasionally gasoline, if several trips are required. The homeowner is encouraged rather to make a donation to the church. The most common problems are clogged garbage disposals, leaky faucets, and balky garage door openers.

"It's rewarding to help someone who's confused about what to do next," Holman adds. "Widows particularly depend on us. We take the place of husbands or sons who aren't there. This is our way of serving the body of Christ."

A Fragrant Offering

East Naples Baptist Church in Florida probably sends flowers to more sick people for less money than any church in the country.

That's because Marie Weedon, a seventyish member of the flower committee, does double duty. She not only helps schedule people to donate a fresh floral arrangement for the altar each Sunday; she also takes it home after the evening service for recycling. The next morning, she divides it up into four or five smaller bouquets and then sets out to deliver them.

"I go to the hospital to see members and friends of members, and I stop at homes where people are sick, too," she says. "They're always so pleased to receive the arrangement. I attach a little card that says, 'These flowers have been on the altar of our church. They have heard the hymns, the prayers, and the sermon, and now they bring their silent message to you with best wishes and love.' "

Weedon has been making her rounds each Monday for three years now, and some have been so impressed with her kindness that they've come to join the church. "I call Monday my sunshine day," she says with a twinkle. "I love it."

A Mission Trip for 70-year-olds

Are service expeditions only for the young? Not according to the senior adult fellowship at First Baptist Church, Gainesville, Florida.

These men and women, each between 70 and 75 years old, were a little tired of the same old activities. One woman said, "You know, I've always wanted to go on a mission. But I've never had the opportunity."

So the group, under the supervision of David Smith, minister with senior adults, wrote to their home mission board in Atlanta. The board responded by putting them in touch with the pastor of Temple Church, Moundsville, West Virginia, a fellowship needing help to finish its new building.

The senior adults took an inventory of what they felt they were good at and contacted the church.

At their own expense, the seniors purchased windows, loaded them in a U-Haul trailer, and headed north. Most of the 11 senior adults rode in the church van, but one man drove his car in case anything went wrong.

After traveling three days at a leisurely pace, they arrived on a Saturday evening in Moundsville. They stayed in a cabin near the new church.

Sunday morning found them in church, and on Sunday night they were given charge of the entire service. They led singing and shared testimonies. Later, they enjoyed fellowship with members of the church.

From Monday to Thursday, they worked hard, hanging windows, painting, and installing insulation. "No one had trouble sleeping those four nights," says David Smith. "After the work was done, we'd go back to our cabin like a big, happy family."

Several people from the Moundsville congregation spoke about how moved they were that a group of senior adults would come so far to serve another church. One man on crutches said it was the best treat he had on memory.

When the van was being fueled up for the trip home, one from the senior adult fellowship told Smith, "This has been the best week of my life. Coming up here, helping these people, and listening to their testimonies has made this event very special to me."

The missions trip cost each senior about $100. "But the money hasn't discouraged any of them," says Smith. "They're chomping at the bit to get away and do it again."

Demythologizing Cancer

While some older adults may wish to avoid the subject, a group of elderly Houstonians is facing cancer head-on by ministering to its victims.

The 20 or so volunteers from South Main Baptist Church focus on a cancer hospital in the nearby Texas Medical Center complex. Each Tuesday they get a computer print-out of new patients, mark the names of (a) those who have signed in as Baptists and are (b) from 100 or more miles away. Then they make assignments. "We want to help those whose family and friends are least likely to be able to come all the way to Houston to visit," explains Linda Jones, minister to senior adults.

The group, called "Friends 'n Deeds," does four things:

• Visits each patient each week.

• Adopts patients with special needs, as identified by the hospital's social service office. Volunteers do their shopping, laundry, make airport trips.

• Find donors to give blood platelets for patients without relatives or friends to call on.

• Maintains Sojourn House, a 10-unit apartment building where outpatients and/or visiting family members can stay at low rates. "Radiation treatments, for example, can drag on for weeks," says Jones, "and patients feel well enough to be out of the hospital — but they can't leave town. Relatives want to be with them. So we let people pack in as many as they wish." Sojourn House is managed by a 70-year-old member who has cancer himself.

The outreach was started by a woman in the church whose friend had cancer. The volunteers meet once a month to update and support each other, report on changing hospital regulations, discuss resource books, and receive training.

"This gives purpose to the lives of our people," says Jones. "It's very rewarding for them. And a good thing is this: they learn that not everyone with cancer dies. Some do go into remission."

Project YOU
(Young and Old United)

Some of life's most touching moments are when those at opposite ends of the age scale intermingle. Here, from three widely scattered churches, are examples:

For two summers in a row, the grade schoolers of First United Methodist Church of Ashland, Kentucky, have raised vegatables to take to elderly members.

"It's hard to teach a child about service without that child being directly involved in serving other people," says Glenna Daut Fay, director of Christian education and leadership training. That's why she arranged for kids to use the garden of a recent widow to raise lettuce, beans, tomatoes, cucumbers, and even flowers. ("The woman was feeling bad," Fay adds, "about having no garden this year since her husband died. She was thrilled to have us take it over, and after our five-week project ended, she gleaned whatever else ripened.")

Fay learned the first time around, in 1981, to choose fast-growing produce: corn was eliminated, for example. Radishes proved too hard for the older adults to eat.

Weeding, harvesting, and delivery took place each Wednesday throughout the early summer. "Actually, the food was just a pretext for interaction," says Fay. "The visiting meant more than the vegetables. But the vegetables gave the kids something to talk about when they went to visit the elderly. There was an immediate bond between them."

The first year Dolores Walker taught fifth and sixth graders at Pioneer United Methodist Chutch in Walla Walla, Washington, she had no teaching partner. "I was on my own, and I felt the weight of nurturing those precious children," she remembers.

So she approached the Rileys, a couple in their seventies who had raised eight children and had 35 grandchildren. They were spry enough, however, to keep up their own ranch and sing in the church choir. Would they serve as class grandparents?

They responded with delight.

"The next Sunday, I told my class what I had done, but without naming the couple. For several weeks I gave clues until they finally solved the mystery.

"The Rileys prayed for us, I know, but they did more. One Sunday they attended class and told us what Sunday school and church were like when they were youngsters. As the year ended, Mrs. Riley invited the class to the ranch for a feast, complete with water goblets and cloth napkins. There was more delicious chicken than even our hungriest boy could hold! The children talk about it still."

A block and a half from First Congregational Church in Downers Grove, Illinois, sits the Immanuel United Church Residence, home for 200 retirees. Once a month or so, the three- and four-year-olds in the church's day care center pack up their storybooks and trot down the sidewalk to "go see the grandmas" for reading time.

"It's only for 45 minutes," says Bill Hoglund, chaplain of the residence and a former staff pastor at the church, "but the impact on the elderly is powerful. To sit and hold a preschooler on your lap and read a story together . . . it often brings tears to their eyes. Sometimes the simplest things have resounding theological impact."

As the children pack up to leave, Hoglund regularly hears a chorus of comments, from "This is a good way to stay young" to "Isn't it great to spoil them — and then let them go home?"

The Telecare Club

Many churches are finding that the most effective ministries to the elderly are the ones planned and implemented by the elderly themselves.

The Telecare Club is a group of elderly persons at Hanover Christian Church in Richmond, Virginia. Periodically, they send out a letter explaining Telecare to elderly persons in the community.

The letter features a big picture of a telephone and the caption: "Live Alone? Who Cares?"

It explains that every day of the year representatives from the church are at the telephone from nine to twelve noon. The church has three lines for this purpose.

Those who belong to the Telecare Club report in every day by phone and usually chat a few minutes. If someone has not been checked off the master list by noon, one of the phone volunteers calls to check on the situation.

When people inquire about Telecare, volunteers send a membership information form to each person. Besides requesting name, address, and phone number, the forms also ask for the names of a close neighbor, a relative, a physician, and pastor, and a caseworker. Further questions include: Do you have a car? What persons have a key to your apartment? What is your physical condition? Is there anything else you would like us to know that would help us be of service to you?

After the forms are returned, the Telecare volunteers file them by name. As members begin to phone in each day, the telephone answerers talk with them a few minutes, listening and encouraging. Pastor Robert W. Maphis, originator and overseer of Telecare, advises the volunteers to be warm and friendly and to be cautious in kidding with the callers. "Since they can't see your face, they may not understand," he says.

If a member doesn't phone in, a phone volunteer

will try to call that person. If there's an emergency or no answer, the volunteer will pull the member's file and contact a neighbor or relative who can look into the situation.

Once, an elderly woman had a heart attack, and it was a phone volunteer who contacted relatives. Another time a furnace duct fell out of the ceiling of an elderly person's home, and Telecare quickly contacted a repair person for help.

"Most of the time," says Maphis, "there is no serious emergency. We just provide a caring ministry to the elderly of our community, from the elderly in our church. I don't know who gets blessed more."

Shut-in but not Shut Out

Must shut-ins be only on the receiving end of minstry?

Faith Lutheran Church in Jackson, Ohio, has discovered that people have a lot to give even when confined to a nursing home.

Isabelle Fisher, for example, taught Sunday school for years until multiple sclerosis struck, and she lost the use of her legs. She had to move into a nursing home, but Isabelle's fingers remained nimble enough for her intricate needlework — and her voice remained strong.

Though she appreciated the tape recordings of the Sunday services, she told Pastor Robert Johnson that she missed participating.

"Isabelle," he said, "how would you like to record the Gospel and Epistle lessons for next Sunday, and we'll play them at church? That way you can be with us." She was delighted.

On Sunday the congregation broke into smiles when they heard Isabelle's clear voice reading the Scripture. Since then she has become one of the regular lectors, taking her turn twice a year. When another member recently had to enter a nursing home, she also became a "recording lector."

"We have about 70 on Sunday mornings," says Johnson, "and in former years I've served larger congregations. But I was far less aware of the resources available from folks who can't sit in the pews, yet are an important part of our congregation.

"I'm thankful our Lord helped us make this discovery."
Reported by Mildred Tengbom

Ma Bell's Call to Worship

Each Sunday, Pastor John Schaumburg makes a phone call and brings another person into the worship service. The person may be hospitalized, shut in, or simply unable to attend that Sunday, but he or she joins the worship at Our Redeemer Lutheran Church in Simi Valley, California — thanks to the phone company and the electronic wizardry of some church members.

"Our congregation has several people who enjoy electronics," says Schaumburg. "And I want people to use their talents within the church whenever possible. So when a faithful member came down with cancer and was unable to attend services, I asked if there was any way to set up a speaker in her room and transmit the worship service to her via the phone."

One man created a homemade device that connects the sanctuary speakers with the office phone. Thanks to a simple on/off switch and Bell's conference calling feature, the worship service can be sent to two homes at once.

"We have a schematic of the device that we gladly furnish on request," says Schaumburg.

"We could send services to people on cassette tape,"

he says. "But we see this as another option — one that allows people to worship with us simultaneously. It's a bridge that keeps people feeling a part of us until they're able to attend again.

"The only thing we haven't figured out," says Schaumburg with a grin, "is how to collect the offering over the phone."

The Communion of Elder Saints

Why should members miss Communion just because they aren't mobile? The elderly and shut-in are often shut out of the Lord's Supper. Here's how two churches remember all of Christ's body.

On the last Wednesday of each month, 25-30 older members of St. Mark's Lutheran Church in Rochester, New York, gather for their 11 A.M. "Communion fellowship."

Church staff and volunteers pick up the shut-ins and bring them to the church fellowship hall, which is accessible to wheelchairs.

After feeding on God's Word and observing the Lord's Supper — led by Pastor Martin Teske — they enjoy refreshments and conversation, catching up on one another's lives and news in the life of the church.

One retired woman, who brings her 99-year-old mother to the group, says she appreciates three things:

● "It's a good hour — it's harder to get ready for an earlier service.

● "It's not too large a crowd — too many people can make older folks nervous.

● "It gives Mother a chance to be with people she knows and enjoys; otherwise it's easy for shut-ins to lose contact with friends their own age."

Jessie O'Dell, volunteer coordinator for the elderly ministry, says, "I'm rapidly working myself out of a job." Group members themselves now phone everyone to coordinate rides and refreshments.

Even those who regularly attend church say they enjoy the Communion fellowship. "It's more relaxed," says one. "There's more time to share things with one another than on Sunday morning."

Adapted from Wheat Ridge Newsletter

At Cairo Baptist Church in southern Illinois, the approach is: If you can't come to Communion, we'll bring Communion to you. After seven years of taking the bread and cup to each shut-in on Sunday afternoon, Pastor Larry Potts decided to have the shut-ins participate in the morning — the same time as everyone else.

"Since our service is broadcast each week, our shut-ins are able to hear the service," says Potts. "But extending our voices is better if we extend our hands, too."

So for the past two years, deaconesses spend Communion Sunday morning with each of the nine permanent shut-ins, plus anyone else who is in the hospital or ill at home.

"We average 12 of these visits during each of our quarterly Communion services," says Potts.

The deaconess and shut-in listen to the service together and then serve one another the Lord's Supper. "We miss the deaconesses on Sunday morning, but their ministry creates a good bond and lets shut-ins know we haven't forgotten them," says Potts.

"A person alone can hear the same words, music, Scripture, but the meaning of Communion is greatly heightened when another believer is present."

See What He Means?

What's the secret of effective speaking to an elderly audience?

J. Grant Swank, Jr., who takes a group from his congregation (Church of the Nazarene, Walpole, Massachusetts) to a nursing home twice a month, says, "Never preach a conventional sermon. Use visual aids as much as possible."

Why? Because those who attend a chapel service, though favorable to spiritual things, are often not as alert as the worshipers on Sunday morning. "Either because of senility or medication, the majority can't stick with a formal, three-point presentation," says Pastor Swank. "In some ways it's like teaching a class of third and fourth graders — you have to involve more of the senses."

Swank sometimes brings his props with him — a cup, a flashlight — but often he makes use of what is already in the room. A floral arrangement gives rise to the sharing of memories about how residents used to raise their own flowers, and the pastor then goes on to talk about God's care for the Christian. One time he picked up a candle, commented on its beauty, but then noted that it was useless if not lit. In the same way, our lives don't shed light to others unless quickened by the Holy Spirit.

Even a blanket or shawl helped introduce a meditation on God's warmth and protection. The ultimate visual experience, Swank has found, is Communion.

"When you give the elderly something to focus their eyes on," he says, "you form an invisible rail on which the spoken word can travel. This fits with what gerontology is now calling 'reality therapy,' in which nursing homes will do things like post the day of the week and the date on a wall in very large letters, just to keep residents in touch with the real world."

As a result of Swank's visuals, communication in his services is often two-way, him asking questions and the audience answering back. Each service also includes mass recitations of Psalm 23, and at the end, the Lord's Prayer.

Never Too Old to Learn

Nursing home ministry works best in the afternoon — correct?

For years the Altoona, Iowa, Regular Baptist Church has successfully held an extension class on Sunday morning at a nearby home for the elderly, sending a teacher, a pianist, and a helper each week. The class, which averages 30 students, is counted as part of the overall Sunday school attendance and uses regular Sunday school curriculum.

"We keep the class to 40 minutes — a little shorter than the classes at church," says Gary Stafford, teacher until recently, "so we have time to get back for the morning worship service. We open with singing, using large-print songbooks, and then go right into the lesson."

The advantages are several:

• Workers are more faithful, since this is the usual time of the week for church ministry. A Sunday afternoon assignment, by contrast, would mean giving up the football game (or your nap).

• The seniors are fresher in the morning as well.

• Real learning takes place — not just the endless comfort and inspiration of most nursing home services.

• The class is an integral element of the church. "It's a blessing to the older saints and also has an evangelistic outreach at the home," says Stafford. "These people really have a sense that they are part of a larger congregation."

A Harvest of Years

Harvest celebrations usually focus on pumpkins, corn, and other edibles. But one year's annual Harvest Heritage Sunday at Oak Grove Mennonite Church in Smithville, Ohio, focused on a different kind of bounty — a "Harvest of Years," honoring the 30 members of the church who were 80 years and older.

Many of our new families didn't know the tremendous contributions of older members," says Pastor Peter Wiebe. "We wanted to honor the aged and let people learn about their lifestyle."

The worship service began with each person over 80 receiving a corsage. Children marched in with the flowers and presented them to 30 "affirmants" (a friend, neighbor, or relative who could introduce and affirm the older person). The affirmants pinned the corsages on the honored aged.

Since eight of the 30 were in rest homes and unable to attend, their affirmants gave 1½-minute introductions to acquaint the congregation with those no longer active.

"I preached on some of the Bible's older people — Abraham and Moses," says Wiebe. "I pointed out that we can still look to older people for wisdom and counsel. We're not just a *now* church." A special table displayed crafts and hobbies of the older folks — needlework, wood crafts, a collection of stones.

After church came a dinner and program of affirmation. Each affirmant told about the older person's contribution to the church and his or her current interests.

The Harvest has had a lasting effect. "Since that Sunday," says Wiebe, "I've noticed the older people, who always sat at the same place near the front, are now sitting with their affirmants. That Sunday helped us bridge the generational gap."

An Object Lesson for the Dying

How do you touch the spirit of a terminally ill person?

James Schackel, pastor of Zion Lutheran Church in Montrose, Colorado, was ministering one Christmastime to a man dying of cancer. As Schackel sought for a symbol of resurrection and hope, he thought about bringing some hyacinth bulbs that were being forced to bloom out of season, in the winter.

"It became a joy to visit this man and his wife and see how the hyacinth bulbs were doing," Schackel reports. "We'd talk about what progress they were making day after day, and it gave me the opportunity to discuss 1 Corinthians 15:35 and the passage that follows. As the hyacinths burst forth, we talked about the fact that 'so it will be with the resurrection of the dead' (v. 42)."

In the weeks that passed before the man's death in early March, the bulbs continued to be a source of conversation and comfort whenever the pastor came to visit. "It gave all three of us something to focus on as we came to terms with the inevitable and began to work through our grieving."

DATE DUE

DEMCO 38-297